LASCAUX
A WORK OF MEMORY

Layout : Sophie Clavel

Isbn 2-86577-232-2

ISBN : 2-86577-237-3

Ouvrage publié avec le concours du Ministère français chargé de la culture - Centre National du Livre

Book published with the support of the French Ministry of Culture - The Book National Center

Jean-Michel Geneste, Tristan Hordé, Chantal Tanet

LASCAUX
A WORK OF MEMORY

Translated by David and Nicole Ball

Preface
Philippe Dagen

FANLAC

CONTENTS

FOREWORD

AT THE ORIGIN of a book there is always a desire to pass something on, and that holds true for this *Lascaux*, the work of six hands. But why did a prehistorian specializing in the Paleolithic and the curator of the Lascaux Cave (Jean-Michel Geneste), and two historians of language and authors of dictionaries (Tristan Hordé and Chantal Tanet) decide to pool their thoughts? A chance encounter in the Vézère Valley in 2000, where we all have close ties, led us to discover similar interests in the process of cultural transmission and in the problems of memory and time in art and language. Our exchanges led to many conversations, which in turn gave us the desire to put them into written form. This is how *Lascaux: A Work of Memory* was born.

The authors,
April, 2003

We wish to thank
Philippe Dagen for the preface,
Direction régionale des Affaires culturelles and Service régional de l'Archéologie (SRA) for their gracious permission to use photographs of Lascaux, and particularly Jean-Paul Lhomme, of the SRA.

PREFACE

Writing about Lascaux is a terrifying exercise.

There is the crushing fame of the cave and its paintings. For most people, they *are* prehistoric art, despite everything that has been discovered before and since (portable objects and wall paintings)—its quintessence, its masterpiece, its definition. There are the books that have been published since the discovery: the many works of the prehistorians, from Abbé Breuil to André Leroi-Gourhan, and the philosopher Georges Bataille's *Lascaux or the Birth of Art*, unique in its genre. There is the profusion of interpretations: although they often tend in the same direction (magic, shamanism), they differ in nuances of vocabulary or points of methodology. Some interpretations rely on comparative studies and ethnology, ignoring the objections that Bataille formulated against such assimilation; others recall models taken from semiology, running the risk of forcing a method of reading on representations that have nothing to do with reading and should not be taken as the equivalent of a text, with its vocabulary, grammar and logic.

And, heading all the reasons not to write about Lascaux anymore, there is the extreme difficulty of the enterprise. It can only be attempted by multiplying precautions, verifying every analytic instrument, and steeling oneself against all temptations to generalize or simplify. Every word, every notion is subject to caution; every single one must be thought through before being put forward. Lascaux is so far removed in time, there are so many gaps in our knowledge, our efforts to imagine it are so suspect that the mind is faced with one of the riskiest adventures it may dare to undertake.

At no point do the authors of *Lascaux, A Work of Memory* forget the extent of the challenge or its difficulty. So the first virtue of their work may be defined negatively: they have resisted all the temptations we have just enumerated and refused to rush into theories or conclusions. While they obviously are familiar with all that has been written about Lascaux, they base what they say only on what can be observed in the cave—on all that can be observed, for it would have been unacceptable to select some information at the expense of other data, judged as negligible or useless. And judged by what criteria? By unexamined assumptions or the hope of defending a pre-established system; in that case, observation would be predetermined by what it had to prove, and would have no value. In the present work, all branches of knowledge are put to use: the geomorphology of the hill and the cavity, chemistry applied to the problem of dating, meticulous examination of the walls, equally precise archaeological study of what excavations have exhumed (used scrapers, spears, lamps)—the complete inventory of what was engraved or painted in the different zones of the cave and the inventory of painting and engraving techniques, so different from one spot to another.

Nothing is insignificant in their remarks. They are meant to stimulate thought, starting with the ones that seem the simplest; they remain unnoticed, and aren't usually taken into account for that very reason.

Take the location of the cave. When Lascaux was occupied in the Magdalenian era, it was an easily accessible cave: it opens onto a gentle hill and it is composed of a few shallow galleries that are not labyrinthine in the slightest. Except for the Shaft, there is nothing hidden, nothing secret about it. At the time it received its paintings, it did not hide them from view—unlike the Cussac cave, for example, which was almost certainly walled in by the same men who worked in it, or Rouffignac, where the works of art are extremely far from the entrance. This comparison would not be sufficient to establish a typology which would depend on distinctions between the degrees of convenience of the cavities and the visibility of the paintings and engravings. In order for such a typology to be constructed, it would have to be developed and refined: for each cave, one would have to know exactly how it looked during the Upper Paleolithic. But now that the idea has been put forth, it can be fertile: Lascaux was an easy, open cave. Should we deduce that it held a central place in some social or religious structure that organized a human group settled nearby? And that this structure must have been obvious, not hidden?

An observation of a quite different nature comes from the analysis of artistic techniques in relation to the nature of the support. Clay calls for tracing with a finger or stick, leaving a furrow in the flexible material. Rough, hard calcite makes it necessary for the paint to be spit or blown out. Depending on its hardness, homogeneity, the presence or absence of flint chunks, cracks and other rough spots, limestone pretty much invites the artist to cut into it with a sharpened point or make a kind of drawing/painting that defines outlines and volumes by modulations of line and color. Clearly the colors of the paint must be characterized as much by their mineral and organic components as by the frequency with which they are used and sometimes by their association with this or that kind of "subject"—a word that should be used prudently. By mapping out this data and counting whatever can be counted, one can see that the Lascaux artists knew how to adjust their technique exactly to the support, although we cannot go further and affirm that this adaptive capacity can be explained by previous experiments. For it would be premature to conclude that willed elaboration and transmission of painting skills existed in the Magdalenian—skills supposedly known only to a few men. Did these populations have individuals whose function it was to paint and engrave in the caves, with all that such specialization presupposes in terms of social organization?

Examination of the material conditions also suggests that the artists overcame difficulties of execution caused by the height of the walls and the darkness of the cave, probably by helping each other with the height and increasing the number of lamps. Thus these remarks lead us to think that their artistic creation was organized—rationally and probably collectively organized: the comparison ventured by Abbé Breuil is thus rather ill-founded, and there was probably no Michelangelo demanding to work alone on the ceiling of the Sistine Chapel, but a group. We know nothing about the number, age, or gender of this group, but we can see that it contained individuals capable of varying their techniques according to the demands of the underground wall.

They were also capable of taking advantage of circumstances. First of all, the special qualities of the stone: in Lascaux, as in most decorated caves, it sometimes seems that this or that motif was suggested by the line of a crack, a rounded bulge or hollow. "Seems," for it is impossible to be certain. Either this is the way it was, and in that case, a few thousand years before Leonardo's lesson, the Paleolithic painters saw forms coming out of the rock and sometimes merely completed, we might say, what nature had already sketched: the outline of a spine, the movement of a snout, the curve of a neck. Or else there is another hypothesis: they searched until they found the spot in the gallery where the animal they wanted to depict would be perfectly in its place and best sustained by the rocky support. One way or the other, the harmony between natural accident and figurative invention does give birth to the work of art. Such harmony, recognized by visual intelligence, proved its effectiveness for the first time in Lascaux.

This intelligence knew how to play with light, too. "Paleolithic light is three-dimensional by nature," as the authors point out: it does not have the even lighting tourists are used to, the lighting dangerously popularized by photographic reproductions. Lamps only give out moving, insufficient gleams, unable to reveal the totality of a whole. In other words, as short separate sequences and not like the friezes stretching out over several meters that we admire today. This mode of perception, so different from our own, deserves a more thorough analysis, as the questions are complex: did this fragmented perception go along with a narrative, or at least were the figures meant to appear in a specific order? In that case, how are we to know in what order, cadence and rhythm we should see the cave in order to recover the gaze of Paleolithic people, if only partially? And what about the painters? Did they have a fragmented vision of their creation or did they multiply their light sources so that they could work on a vast surface, a room, ceiling, or gallery? Unfortunately, we will never know. But at least the questioning has begun; it breaks our present habits of reproduction, which spoil our studies methodologically by giving them documents that are all too complete.

This holds true for those tricky problems of interpretation: they are a long way from being solved. Often there are no answers. But the absence of answers and the awareness of uncertainty is better than false certainties accepted out of laziness or habit. A methodical description of Lascaux does not allow us to discover systematic connections between a given animal motif and a color, nor between a given motif and a technique, nor to note the recurrence of an association to which we might be tempted to attribute some symbolic function—despite what Leroi-Gourhan thought he saw. No element gives us the right to proceed in this direction. Not one really helps in decoding the animal groups or the enigmatic Shaft Scene and the geometric pictograms that are usually thought to be "signs"—which is already saying too much, since "sign" implies the inscription of one or several meanings in a stable form, as in Egyptian hieroglyphics. At this point in the book, the authors probably felt the temptation to go further and venture a few elements of interpretation in their turn. Methodological scruples held them back. They did not abandon their usual care for precision: they first chose to remind us of what had been written about a painting—the Shaft Scene for example—not to refute some thesis, but to show how impossible it is to reach a conclusion, how preferable to let these images retain their elusive polysemy, their enigmas.

This does not prevent them from formulating with unusual clarity a number of observations that deal with what one may suppose about the relationship between these representations and the context of their execution. First of all, this observation: animal motifs are largely predominant in Lascaux as in all decorated caves, and this predominance must have a connection to the hunter-gatherers' way of life, closely dependent on their knowledge of prey, places and seasons. The precision of line and the accuracy of postures cannot be separated from the actual experience of the hunters; they require the same qualities of vision, memory and gesture. As Ernst Grosse pointed out at the end of the nineteenth century, the particular quality of the paintings indicates that they could only have been the work of men used to tracking down their prey. Evoking "elements of actual experience and the memory of experience" means, in different words from those of the German anthropologist, recalling how intense the relation was between these representations and the conditions of life—which does not necessarily mean assuming magic ceremonies or propitiatory cults.

Another remark lends itself to intellectual speculation: "men would move along under a painted vault, almost on their hands and knees, more or less as they did in Font-de-Gaume. They would thus be moving through a narrow passage, a womb-like universe, forced to bow down under the artworks. Symbolically this is not without meaning." Not without meaning indeed, but ambiguous: in that abundance of images, that bent posture, should we recognize a sign of the strong authority the representation had for them, forcing them to bow down before it in a gesture of respect or devotion? Or a sign of such familiarity that man connected with animal in the darkness, and for a moment, animal and man became one, so to speak? In other words, was this veneration or communion? At this stage, our thought moves along one of the most uncertain and shifting lines there is, the line that might separate humanity from animality, that might circumscribe the unique nature of man. But what "nature" and defined in what way, if not by today's thinking, produced in circumstances and with the information and logic we have now, which is definitively, inescapably different from theirs? This "unique nature" as we think of it today is a superiority—an obviously dominant position, since men have subjugated animals for thousands of years, and recently even mastered their genetic codes in order to transform them. But at the time of Lascaux? Nothing shows it was the same, everything suggests things were different. Did man feel so different from the animals his survival depended on, from those beasts that could defeat and kill him—sometimes devour him—just as he himself could defeat and devour them? Did he want to make sure he had a fruitful hunt through his paintings, or reduce the distance that was increasingly separating him from all other living creatures? Was he trying to appease them, to be accepted by them, to join them?

As we follow this hypothesis, we soon hit upon this paradox: the art of the people of Lascaux, which sets them absolutely apart from the human beings who preceded them for millions of years, may be the decisive sign of their humanity as well as a kind of temptation to animality. They attempt to approach the rest of living creatures—horse, aurochs, bison. Yet simultaneously and decisively, that same gesture shows their definitive break from animality. For they know how to depict, that is, to objectify sensations, and they can organize the process at the end of which engraved or painted figures appear—organize, and thus reproduce them.

The birth of art, to use Georges Bataille's expression, may thus be the moment when man perceives himself as man, and at the same time, necessarily, the moment he feels that he will no longer be an animal—with all the emotion, anxiety and regret that goes along with such a break. In other words, art, at its beginnings (and perhaps occasionally again in its history, but in spasms, flashes) may be the ephemeral moment of "alliance" between humanity and animality, the last animality of man and also the way of staving off inhumanity—the rationalization of the birth and death of his fellow men—which characterizes societies since the end of the nineteenth century.

Nowhere is this alliance more intense than at Lascaux.

Philippe Dagen

Professor of Art History, Université Paris I Panthéon-Sorbonne

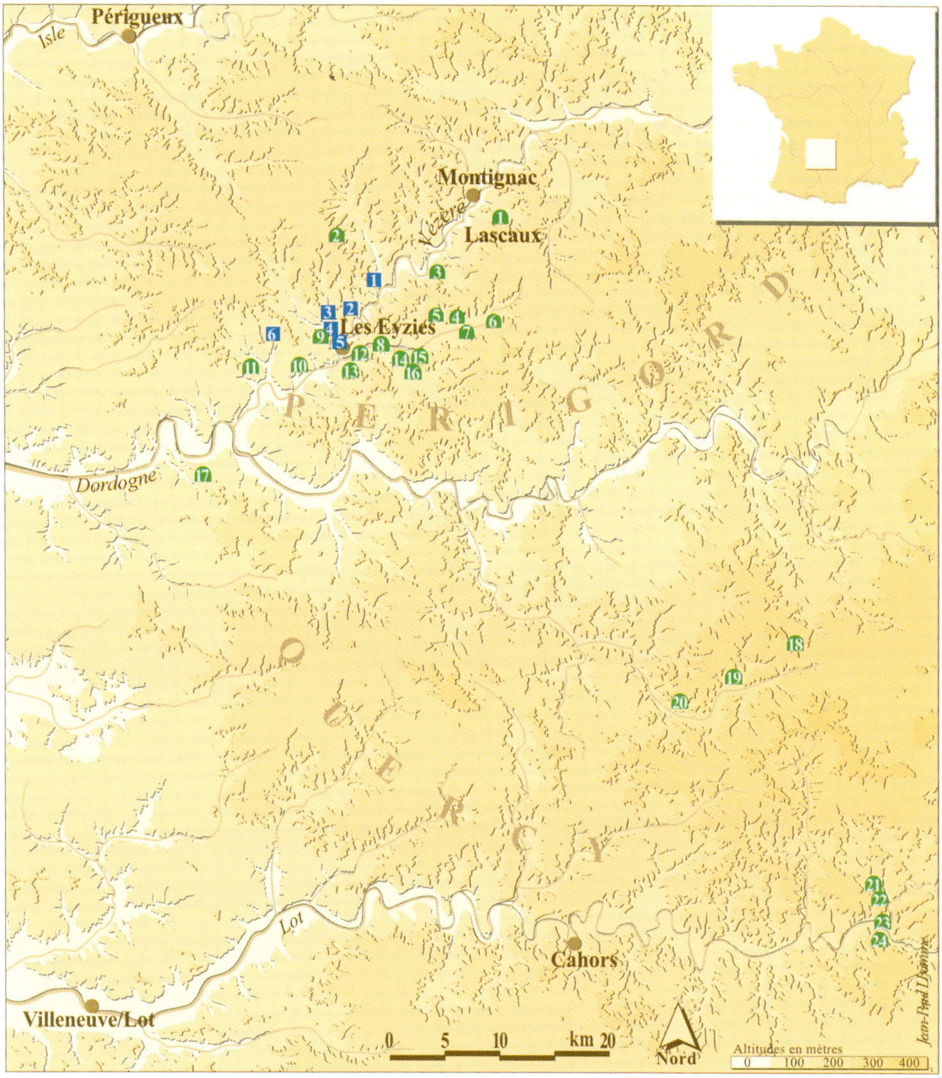

DECORATED CAVES AND SHELTERS: 1 Lascaux, 2 Rouffignac, 3 Les Roches (the Reverdit, Labattut, Blanchard and Castanet shelters), 4 Cap-Blanc shelter, 5 La Grèze Cave, 6 Laussel shelter, 7 Comarque, 8 Les Combarelles I and II, 9 Gorge d'Enfer valley (Poisson shelter, Oreille d'Enfer Cave), 10 Saint-Cirq, 11 Bara-bahau, 12 Font-de-Gaume, 13 La Mouthe, 14 La Calévie, 15 Nancy, 16 Bernifal, 17 Cussac, 18 Fieux, 19 Les Merveilles, 20 Cougnac, 21 Marcenac, 22 Pech-Merle, 23 Christian, 24 Le Moulin.

DEPOSITS: 1 Le Moustier, 2 La Madeleine, 3 La Micoque, 4 Laugerie-Haute and Basse, 5 Vignaud and Pataud, 6 La Ferrassie.

THE UPPER PALEOLITHIC IN WESTERN EUROPE

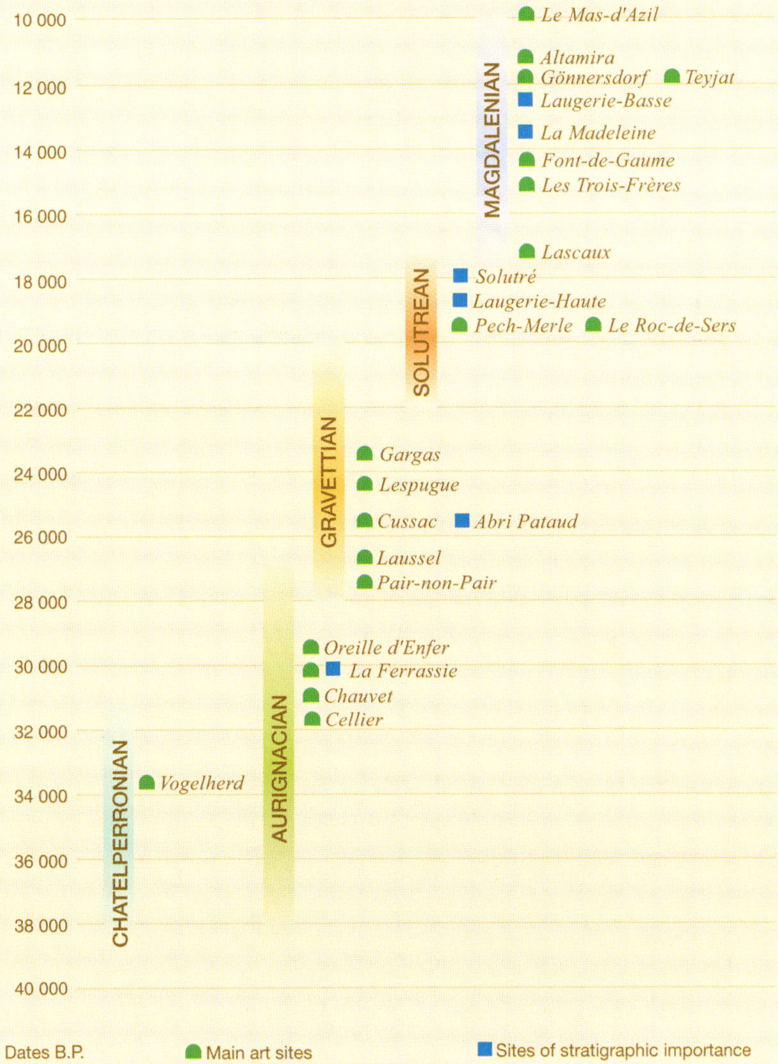

Jean-Paul Lhomme

MAP OF THE CAVE

INTRODUCTION

FOR millions of years, human beings continued to follow the paths leading to certain caves and shelters decorated by the Paleolithic hunters. But for a very long time, they could not even imagine that these far-off ancestors ever existed or recognize the deposits they had left behind. Besides, what remains of these societies that occupied the territory of Europe for hundreds of centuries? The fragments left by their social activities are more numerous than is sometimes thought, but still too scarce to enable us to write their history. For the human beings who lived at the time of the Chauvet Cave, or nearer to us, Lascaux, archeologists analyze the rare sepultures that have been preserved, the remains of their camps, their painted and engraved walls, their sculpture. They classify thousands of tools and objects accumulated from their excavations or brought to light by farm work, the opening of a sandpit or digging for a new road. They can determine the origin of the materials prehistoric populations used and where they went to find them. They can reconstruct their plant environment by studying the pollen still present in the ground, partially describe their food from the animal bones abandoned near their habitats; they even know some of the illnesses they suffered from. All this research has almost entirely erased the longstanding image of Neanderthals and Cro-Magnons as humans close to the animal state. But the places and objects of prehistoric times remain silent on many points: there are far more hypotheses than established certainties.

From the eighteenth century on, the long-broken thread of memory has slowly been knotted together again, from stones to animal and human bones, from bones to carved objects, and then to engraved and painted walls. As these vestiges were gradually uncovered and gradually attributed to the time before written history, they changed the way we think of the past. Indeed, these discoveries progressively pushed back the time human beings appeared on earth: at the beginning of the nineteenth century, it was estimated at approximately 5,000 years before our era, a century later it still was thought to coincide "with the beginning of the Quaternary, at least 230-240,000 years ago" (G. and A. Mortillet, *La Préhistoire*, 1910); today we speak of over four million years.

Changes in the way we perceive human beings and their activities have also been important. For prehistorians of the early twentieth century, on the one hand the Neanderthal type "slowly modified and developed all through the old Quaternary, ending up in the Cro-Magnon type" and, on the other hand, when they worked in bone or painted a wall, "men of this era were flighty, lacking in reflection and foresight" (G. and A. Mortillet, *op. cit.*) Fifty years later, André Leroi-Gourhan strongly affirms: "The painstaking study of the decoration of the caves has led to a veritable rehabilitation of the prehistorian's savage predecessor, the discovery of a rich, coherent figurative system, supple and alive." (*Les Religions de la préhistoire*, 1955.)

Prehistoric men… with no history?

Today it is a proven fact that France, England, etc., even Egypt and Palestine, were haunted for hundreds of thousands of years by savages who painfully acquired the benefits of civilization, and that nowhere did this civilization appear among them spontaneously and all at once. While some peoples,

through their stubborn efforts, attained a certain measure of advanced civilization, others have been unable to discover a means of making fire to this very day. Savage people of our day have no history; neither did prehistoric peoples. For only men with a certain degree of civilization are capable of preserving the memory of historical facts and passing it on to their descendents. Little more than vague echoes of the prehistoric era have come down to us, like the stories of combats waged by primitive man against some of the animals of his time.
Pierre Larousse, *Grand dictionnaire universel du XIXe siècle*, "*Préhistoire*," 1875.

Many sites have been discovered and studied since Larousse, and analytical techniques have been transformed. As for the Lascaux Cave, it changed the way we used to look at Paleolithic art, if only by revealing it to the public at large. Annette Laming-Emperaire, who devoted part of her writing to the cave, wrote in 1959:

> The works of art it contained were among the finest and best preserved that have ever been brought to light. The discovery renewed interest in prehistoric rock art and expanded the circle of its admirers to include a wider audience. (*Lascaux, peintures et gravures.*)

Like others, the decorated cave of Lascaux reveals a burgeoning tangle of juxtaposed, superimposed, overlapping elements (figures and non-figurative representations, paintings and engravings) which defy the quest for all-inclusive, total meaning. Could we reconstruct some kind of narrative from the pictorial groups distributed across the different sectors of the cave? Certainly not. They form a kind of gigantic, three-dimensional jig-saw puzzle whose rules for assembly—elaborated as they were over several thousand years—utterly escape us. But we can indicate the place the cave occupies in the environment, the significance of the cavern, how the whole parietal disposition is constructed, and reflect on the status of painting and engraving, on the functions these artworks had in the societies that brought them into being. This group of questions leads to others, about the origins of art and a society's relationship to the past.

What this settlement of Paleolithic hunters gives us is a work of memory, the traces—still very much alive today—of societies that inscribed a part of their past here. The figures on the walls make up a kind of discontinuous, yet homogeneous collection of symbols, passed on and practically untouched for thousands of years. Even if the questions they raise remain unanswered, the paintings and engravings of Lascaux stir up echoes in many aspects of our social life.

For complex reasons, Lascaux has become a spiritual emblem: for many people, it is indeed the "birthplace" of art, the underground place of our foundations. The forgotten work of memory has been passed on to posterity by means of an incomplete replica (Lascaux II), a place of pilgrimage or quest for origins, a "generic symbol of the undiscoverable prehistoric memory of France." (J.-P. Demoule, *Lascaux*, in *Les France*, 2, 1992.)

FROM MYTH TO PREHISTORY

The Time of Our Origins

For the longest time, human beings have told the circumstances of their appearance on earth in the form of myths, and then what they thought of as an evolution of their species. "One must not forget that our species, *Homo sapiens*, was born about forty thousand years ago and that his birth certificate is signed by the appearance of highly utilitarian objects of curiosity and works of art. Since then, his grasp of the world has always been accompanied by a parallel development of arts and philosophies as elements of equilibrium. That is why asking burning questions about our ancestry and meaning in the living world is as indispensable to us as affirming themselves through artistic expression of their myths was to our distant predecessors." (André Leroi-Gourhan, *Le Fil du temps*, 1983.) Let us reread a few of these mythical constructions of the western world, keeping in mind that they have points in common with those of other civilizations.

In ancient Greece, the development of the human race was imagined as a coherent succession of periods: humanity began by living in a golden age, an age of leisure and abundant food, then experienced a gradual decline in living conditions. This way of reconstructing the time of our origins appears in Greece seven centuries before the Common Era, with the poet Hesiod. It lasted for a very long time, particularly through Roman civilization. At the time of the Emperor Augustus, at the beginning of the first century, the poet Ovid imagined Jupiter's creation of man from a divine seed or by modeling a little bit of clay, and he then describes four ages. The Golden Age was followed by the Silver Age when nature, which used to be static, entered into measurable time: the year was divided into four seasons, men had to work and protect themselves from bad weather. "And then, for the first time, men went into houses; these houses were caves, leafy boughs, and branches mingled with bark." (Ovid, *Metamorphoses*, I.) War between men began in the Bronze Age that followed, and then came the Iron Age, in which we are still living, one of "fraud, perfidy, treason, violence and the evil passion for wealth."

This vision of our origins left traces in literature and painting, but a particular variant, transmitted by the Old Testament, triumphed in the West. A creator made a masculine being out of clay, and from him, pulled a feminine being; both of them, Adam and Eve, were placed in a paradise. In this place, which corresponds to the Golden Age of the Greeks and Romans, the couple had everything they needed and would live for eternity in harmony with all living things. The knowledge of death, that is, of time, came from their disobedience to their creator. Adam and Eve then became aware of their weakness and their nakedness in a universe where nothing was a given any more. Next, the creator decided to do away with humanity, whose faults were growing, in his eyes; to begin a new era, he covered the Earth with the waters of a flood. Only one couple from each living species survived this destruction, in the ark built by Noah.

In the West, the age of humanity was then estimated from the flood related in the biblical text: between 2,800 and 6,000 years before the coming of Christ. For a long time, the length of this time was disputed, but not the way it was calculated. However, certain interpretations of the Bible made it possible to increase the length of time. Thus the idea was put forth in the mid-seventeenth century that the Old Testament told the history of the Hebrew people, not that of humanity, so the notion of *pre-adamic* was suggested: if men lived before Adam, there was no obstacle to setting the moment of their appearance back in time.

The Shattering of Biblical Time

What about fossils? The people of antiquity had already noticed that one could find "sea-shells quite far from the sea and old anchors on mountain tops" (Ovid, *Metamorphoses*, XV), which proved that the sea had covered the earth in a distant era. For Christianity, it was the flood that had left the sea-shells and plants that were discovered in the ground. This point of view was strongly called into question in the eighteenth century and rejected by the Encyclopedists in Diderot's group. They asserted that "without departing from the respect due the testimony of the Scriptures," the thickness of the fossil layers led one to think that the waters of the sea had remained for a number of centuries. And the author of the article *Deluge* added: "Besides, there is no reason not to suppose that the earth may have gone through other upheavals, quite apart from the flood. This said, we have reason to believe that the sea fossils found inside the earth are not the products of the flood that Moses talks about, which was a rather transitory event." (*Deluge*, in Diderot, *Dictionnaire raisonné des arts et des sciences.*) Seventy years later, the great naturalist Georges Cuvier retained that idea of successive upheavals in a theory that enabled him to save the content of the biblical text. According to him, there may have been thousands of centuries of catastrophes, but only five to six thousand years since the last flood related in the biblical text. As a rationalist, he bases his ideas on facts and does not reject the idea that humanity could exist before written history.

Everything leads us to believe that the human species did not exist in the lands where fossils have been discovered at the time of the upheavals that buried these bones (…); but from that I do not mean to conclude that man did not exist at all before that era. He may have inhabited a few small lands, from which he repopulated the earth after those terrible events. (G. Cuvier, *Discours sur les révolutions (…)*, 1812.)

How was the reference-point of the flood abandoned and when, as we emerged from mythical time, did we begin to construct the history of man? The changes in perspective that led to the founding of prehistory were extremely slow.

History before History

Some of the tools left by prehistoric men were known ever since antiquity, but they were not perceived as being made by man. These regularly shaped stones were thought to have been shaped by lightning and magical properties were attributed to this heavenly gift. These "lightning stones," as they were called, were still much sought after well beyond the Middle Ages; they were worn for their supposed medicinal qualities, or else as a good-luck charm.

Stone Implements and Superstition

The weapons and tools of the Stone Age were quickly forgotten once they were no longer used, and supplanted by metal. Afterwards, when they were found, their regular shape and their substance—which differed from that of the surrounding rock—caught people's attention and had to be explained. Meanwhile, lightning had been the object of the religious fears of humanity for a long time. Lightning, which strikes living things dead, smashes all obstacles, burns down houses, rips up trees and disappears into the ground was never understood without some material manifestation. Superstition linked this manifestation to the polished axes, the stone arrowheads that make fire through percussion, all seen and gathered in plowed-up earth, on the ground washed by the rains of a storm.

Add to this the fact that almost everywhere lightning and its effects were always identified with meteors and the results of their fall, and a stone fallen from the sky—a sacred stone—could often be found.

Thus a myth was born, perhaps the oldest and most general myth of all.

Émile Cartailhac, *L'Âge de pierre dans les souvenirs et superstitions populaires,* 1877.

Next, tools and weapons were integrated into acceptable historical frameworks; as they were foreign to Greco-Roman civilization, which was familiar to everyone, they were pronounced Celtic. As time passed, there were hesitations. The archeologist François Jouannet (1765-1845), looking for Gallo-Roman antiquities in Dordogne, discovered the site of Combe-Grenal in 1816, then the site of Pech-de-l'Azé; he attributed the tools and bones associated with those sites to the Celts, but only because he could not imagine another answer:

Here the work of man is evident everywhere, but for what purpose? How far back should we date this barbaric handiwork, this strange deposit? We have no answer, and if we speak of this cave under the rubric of Gallic antiquities it is only because what we saw there bears the stamp of the oldest antiquity. (F. Jouannet, *Antiquités gauloises*, 1818.)

Before that, human bones had been discovered next to fossils of extinct animals. For example, in 1774, the German naturalist Johann Frederick Esper, comparing such remains, had suggested that they belonged to a time before history, earlier than the period of the biblical flood. His proposals were forgotten. In the first years of the nineteenth century, the English geologist William Buckland studied similar material discovered in Wales, along with domestic objects and traces of red ochre on the human bones: he dissociated the animal remains from the human, dating the latter to the Roman conquest.

The turning-point probably came at the beginning of the eighteen-thirties, with the physician Casimir Picard, who set up the first analysis of layers of terrain in Abbeville, while maintaining the division into Celtic, Roman and Medieval eras. Also in Abbeville, Jacques Boucher de Perthes, who was close to Picard, collected polished axes in 1837, stone tools, bones of extinct animals, then a handaxe in 1842, and deep underground, in 1845, an elephant tooth. His analyses, which formed what he called *archeogeology*, were founded on the study of successive layers (in other words, stratigraphy) left by the generations: the ground was considered as a content in itself and the study of each layer restored the history of human beings before the flood. Boucher de Perthes met up with the strongest opposition from practically every member of the Académie des Sciences; yet a few of them came to see his collections and agreed with his conclusions, as did some English scientists. At last, the existence of antediluvian man was officially accepted in France in 1860, after a report by Édouard Lartet, the same man whose discoveries with Henry

Christy at Les Eyzies in Dordogne changed our view of what was now becoming prehistory.

Stratigraphic study and the analysis of stone implements contradicted the idea that man had been created once and for all. It placed him within the framework of time by introducing evolution into tool-making. Man went from simple use of a flint to its transformation by stone-cutting, the use and finishing of stone flakes, and finally to the use of bone after stone. This transformism called into question the dogma of biblical man and led to intense polemics and then to ideological stands that tried to reconcile the text of the Bible and the discoveries of the new discipline.

Original Man According to Rousseau

(...) I will fancy him [man in the state of nature] the same as I see him today, walking on two feet, using his hands as we use ours, looking over all of nature and measuring the vast expanse of the sky with his eyes.

By stripping this being, thus constituted, of all the supernatural gifts he might have received, and of all the artificial faculties that he could only have acquired through long progress; by considering him, in a word, exactly as he must have come from the hands of nature, I see an animal less strong than some, less agile than others, but all things considered, organized more advantageously than all of them: I see him satisfying his hunger under an oak tree, slaking his thirst at the first passing stream, finding his bed at the foot of the same tree that gave him his meal, and thus his needs are satisfied.

The earth, left to its natural fertility and covered with immense forests never mutilated by the axe, offers storehouses at every step and shelters for all kinds of animals. The men scattered among them observe, imitate their industry, and thus raise themselves to the instinct of animals, with the advantage that every species only has its own instinct, whereas man, who perhaps has none that belongs to him, appropriates all of them, and nourishes himself with most of the varied food that other animals share, and thus finds his subsistence more easily than any of them are able to do.

Accustomed from childhood on to bad weather and the rigors of the seasons, accustomed to fatigue, and forced to defend, without weapons, their life and their prey against other ferocious animals, or escape them by running, men forge a robust, almost unchangeable temperament. Children, bringing into the world the excellent constitution of their fathers, and fortifying it through the same exercises that produced it, thus acquire all the vigor of which the human species is capable. Nature (...) makes those who have good constitutions strong and robust, and kills off all the others, differing in that regard from our societies, where the State, by making children a burden to their fathers, kills them off indistinctly before their birth.

Rousseau, *Discours sur l'origine et les fondements de l'inégalité parmi les hommes*, 1755, in *Oeuvres complètes, III*, Gallimard, 1964. (*Discourse on the Origin and Foundations of Inequality among Men.*)

Can Art Exist before History?

It took time for the idea of humanity living before the flood to be accepted. It was impossible for the representations of animals or the signs carved on tools or bones, or on the walls of caves, to be immediately recognized for what they were. At first they were mere curiosities: from the middle of the sixteenth century on, the cave of Rouffignac in Dordogne (called the *Miremont Cave* at the time) was presented as a place to visit for its natural strangeness and for the ancient human and animal traces that could be seen there. Then the animal figures were attributed to the Celts, like the tools: the carving on a bone found in Vienne (Chaffaud Cave) around 1834 was only analyzed in 1869, but its origin was defined as Celtic at that time.

Édouard Lartet's 1861 discovery of the carvings of the heads of a bear and a bird on a deer antler in the cave of Massat in Ariège dramatically raised the question of true artistic production. Still, acknowledging the existence of portable art did not immediately result in a new look at the engravings or paintings in the caves. The wall paintings in Niaux (Ariège) were found in 1864 by the prehistorian Félix Garrigou (1835-1920), but not interpreted; neither were the engravings seen in 1878 in the Chabot Cave (Ardèche) by Léopold Chiron. During the same period, only a few prehistorians like Édouard Piette, who indefatigably worked on-site, accepted the extremely early origin of the bison painted on the ceiling of the Altamira Cave (Spain) discovered in 1879 by Marcelino Sáinz de Sautuola. The scientific community claimed it was a fraud, and one of the arguments of the French specialist who looked at the wall painting clearly shows that the rejection of the facts (that is, the reality of the paintings) depended on prior choices. The paintings were pronounced recent *because* certain techniques *could not have been* known to prehistoric man. Example: bichromia and the lightening of colors, *because* light does not reach the spot where the paintings were discovered (how can you paint without light?), etc.

According to another prehistorian, Gabriel de Mortillet, tools were developed to satisfy new needs, and the weight of such environmental constraints prevented, he claimed, the formation of religious ideas in the Paleolithic era. No religion, no artistic creation.

Thus, for him, the graves discovered in 1861 in Aurignac (Haute-Garonne) and Cro-Magnon (Les Eyzies, Dordogne) in 1868, must have been dug in older layers.

Rock art only became a reality after 1895. In April, four men who were not prehistorians entered La Mouthe Cave in Les Eyzies and discovered engravings a hundred meters from the entrance. Émile Rivière was notified. He had explored that entrance two years earlier, and in June 1895, he authenticated the engravings; they were officially recognized on August 14, 1902. It was also in 1902 that Émile Cartailhac's fine text "*Altamira, mea culpa d'un sceptique*" appeared; he rejects his original refusal to accept the prehistoric art at Altamira and confirms the position of the majority of prehistorians. After that, despite some rear-guard combat, prehistoric art begins to exist.

From then on, the discoveries become more frequent: scholars know what they can find, and the locations charted in previous years are revisited. The problem of lighting is solved when, in August 1899, a sandstone lamp with charcoal deposits is found in La Mouthe Cave. Then scholars remember that similar objects were extracted as early as 1854 from the cave of Chaire-à-Calvin (Charente.) In Les Eyzies, the Combarelles engravings are discovered in 1901, the paintings at Font-de-Gaume the same year, and Abbé Henri Breuil begins listing the artworks in the caves in 1901 as well. Interpretations of rock art are elaborated at the same time. Yet it is only in 1909 that the decorated caves enter officially into the collective memory, when they are classified as historical monuments.

1

HALL OF BULLS

2

4

6

8

13

Hall of Bulls

The rotunda of the Hall of Bulls is covered by one continuous fresco. To the left, a wild dream, the Unicorn, a fantastic animal born from the imagination of its creator, leads the march of the cavalcade. (1)

The whole painting is in the arc of a circle. It surrounds and dominates the observer. Such composition forces him to raise his eyes and pivot on himself to apprehend the whole work. Only the middle band of the wall—an easily accessible overhang covered by an attractive crust of brilliant calcite—has been painted. (2, 3, 4.)

Five large aurochs outlined in black visually dominate this special space in the fresco. Their similar, but highly contrasting heads stand out in the upper band. (5, 6, 7, 8.)

Under the gaze of two huge aurochs a group of five little deer are moving to the left (9.) The animals in the foreground are complete, detailed and contrasted in black, yellow and red (10), whereas the ones in the middle distance have more evanescent and less contrasted silhouettes in light red: only a few discreet graphic elements distinguish them from the relief of the wall (11.)

Lower down, the dark red and black masses of horses, of smaller red aurochs, of a bear, deer, and signs are all tangled together in the midst of the immense bodies of the aurochs and in all the free spaces of the wall painting (12, 13.)

THE LASCAUX CAVE

The Discovery

The Lascaux Cave was brought to light by accident on September 12, 1940, thousands of years after its last phase of occupancy. Almost forty years after the official recognition of rock art, nothing suggested that an important discovery would be made in an area known to have been inhabited ever since the Gallo-Roman era, but with none of the high, rocky cliffs that characterize the region of Les Eyzies. The layman's eye was undoubtedly sensitized by increasing public access to a domain previously limited to specialists and by increasing familiarity with objects and images of the Paleolithic world. After Altamira and La Mouthe, neophytes can see—that is, identify—ornaments on the walls of a cave.

The fact that the discoverers of Lascaux were a quartet of adolescents probably gave a fairy-tale tone to the story of its discovery. It took the curiosity and bold endeavor of an adolescent, who entered a narrow cavity and plunged deep into darkness like the prince of the Perrault fairy-tale breaking the spell that had frozen Sleeping Beauty in a hundred-year sleep, to bring that work—buried for so many thousands of years—to light untouched, directly out of human memory: his fresh but knowledgeable gaze re-inscribed it in historical time. Specialists were informed rather rapidly, and acted a few days later: Abbé Henri Breuil, who was then in Brive at the home of his fellow-scholar Jean Bouyssonnie, got there by September 21.

To this day, the Lascaux Cave is still associated with the people who discovered it—Marcel Ravidat (then eighteen years old), Jacques Marsal, Simon Coencas (aged fifteen) and Georges Agnel (sixteen)—and with the initiatory adventure they shared with their teacher, Léon Laval. As for the little town of Montignac, pulled from its torpor on that day of September 1940, it has remained unknown outside the region: if the name of Lascaux is well known, the name of Montignac is hardly familiar beyond the area, and yet this town controls the access to the site of the cave.

> After crossing the charming little town of Montignac, we are now at the foot of the church of the Prieuré, which seems to forbid access to the famous Lascaux Cave. Let us leave the ancient outlying district of la Pègerie on our left, with its medieval street-stalls; it used to overlook the entrance to the toll for the wooden bridge, which burnt down long ago.
> Rue du Barry, an extremely old street that takes its name from a fortified gate which no longer exists, is located on the site of an old Roman road that used to connect Limoges and Cahors; it takes us, in a few minutes, to the bottom of the rustic, charming hillside that conceals "the eighth wonder of the world."
> Towards the top, a poplar, like a plumed crest, seems to point to the entrance of this mysterious cave. Who would ever have thought that on September 12, 1940, some teenagers vaguely looking for adventure would discover the marvel that was to perpetually pique the interest of tourists and scientists!
> Léon Laval, *La Caverne peinte de Lascaux*, Éditions du Périgord noir, Montignac, 1948.

The authenticity of the decorations found in Lascaux was immediately confirmed by the judgment of specialists, but it was not self-evident for everybody. The Surrealist writer André Breton, for example, still questioned the age of parietal art in general and would move his fingers over the wall paintings, up to the day in 1952 when the guide to the cave of Pech-Merle in Cabreret (Lot) took him to task and pressed charges against him in court. Following this case, the *Société des Gens de Lettres* (Society of Authors) called for an investigation; Henri Breuil rejected this request in a report submitted to the Commission Supérieure des Monuments Historiques[1].

Oddly enough, this argument over the authenticity of the painted works of art continued after the discovery of Altamira, but for quite different reasons. It took all the stubbornness of a few prehistorians like Émile Rivière in La Mouthe (at Les Eyzies) as early as 1893, and then the discoveries of Combarelles and Font-de-Gaume in 1901 to sweep away this scepticism, but outside of the circle of prehistorians, the paintings were often attributed to contemporaries, particularly to draft resisters in Napoleon's First Empire, or even to Abbé Breuil himself. A guide in the Vézère Valley even told his customers that he had seen paint cans behind the entrance to Lascaux...

The Choice of the Site and the Cave

When we travel from cave to cave (...) who among us knows, like Abbé Breuil, that we are following in the footsteps of the Compostella pil-

1 André Breton had to pay a fine. He tried to justify his vandalism. "In 1951, I visited most of the caves in Dordogne (Les Eyzies, Lascaux, etc.). I made a point of verifying for myself the existence of a layer of limestone covering the prehistoric drawings on many occasions, without the slightest conflict between the guide and me." (*Œuvres complètes*, vol. 3, p. 1075, Gallimard, 1999.)

grims and that the roads of medieval pilgrimages had previously been thoroughfares for moving hordes and goods of the Quaternary? (Max Raphaël, *Trois essais sur la signification de l'art pariétal paléolithique.)*

The site of Lascaux is not on the road of some pilgrimage, but it was certainly not by chance that it was chosen for the use that was made of it. The necessity of identifying the place over the course of time through the uncertain means of oral transmission leads us to this essential question: in the Paleolithic context, in the absence of surface inscriptions, how could people orient themselves in the territory? How did they organize themselves mentally?

The hill of Lascaux is neither lost nor hidden in the countryside; it is on a promontory slightly set back from the valley—that is, an easy part of the landscape to spot. Almost all the great sites are located in places easily visible in the landscape, whether one thinks of Altamira, la Roche de Solutré (Saône-et-Loire), the Pech-Merle Cave (Lot), or, in Dordogne, of Font-de-Gaume, Laussel, or the shelters under the great cliff of Les Eyzies such as Pataud, and across from there, the shelters of Laugerie-Basse, which were occupied at every period of the Paleolithic. When people arrived from the west or the east, as they followed the Vézère Valley, they would necessarily find at Les Eyzies the occupied shelters on the right and left-hand banks of the river. These places served as landmarks. The Chauvet Cave can be characterized in the same way: leaving the Rhône valley, you go up the Ardèche River, and when the stream flows under the natural arch of Pont-d'Arc, the cave is located just above it. We do not know exactly where to locate it in the mountain, but if we take the narrow geological traverse path down the cliff, used since the Paleolithic and, in the historic era, followed by shepherds leading their flocks, we necessarily come upon the entrance to the cave, alongside the path that connects the valley to the plateau.

The topographical position of Lascaux on the hill is probably decisive in relation to its contents and the great concentration of caves in the same area. Here as elsewhere, myths need structures to become established. Indeed, there are many examples of ethnic territories set in a natural landscape that use the form of an animal to transcribe their myths—the water-buffalo on the island of Sumba-Wa, for example, or the elephant of the Pygmies of the Tikar basin in Cameroon. This or that feature of the landscape—hill, stream, mountain—is thus named after a part of the animal's anatomy: the ear, the tail, the trunk.

The choice of the site of Lascaux is no more a question of chance than the choice of the cave. The criterion of the cave's orientation, in particular, must have played its part. The cave is practically open to the northwest; its entrance is potentially illuminated at sunset, and more precisely at the summer solstice. If, as one may presume, there was normally a clear entrance five or six meters wide and two meters high in the prehistoric period, the rays of the setting sun were in a direct line from the entrance. The evening light, which is red at the time of the summer solstice, could illuminate and color the Hall of Bulls at the bottom of the incline that led to it.

The underground space of the caves is quite distinct from the space of outdoor camps or rock shelters. Underground space is ill-suited for domestic life because of its darkness; it is full of invisible and thus unthinkable obstacles. And yet some of its characteristics are not necessarily inhospitable. As light accompanies the visitor, the space changes its appearance: in the darkness, the light creates volumes, suggests forms and can animate them by making the visual creations on the walls come alive.

Another factor: temperature remains constant in underground space, as opposed to the outside (it was obviously colder in the glacial period than in a temperate era like our own.) The entrance to the caves was thus a natural refuge for animals (meat-eaters, predators) … and men, all coveting that ecological niche and fighting over it.

The naked footprints of youths on the humid floors observed in a number of decorated cavities clearly show that these deep, secret places were frequently used during the Paleolithic, no matter how difficult it was to get to them. One can recognize human traces and figures on the walls up to the deep end of the underground cavities, which indicates that these spaces were not deemed too inhospitable. Finally, the evocative shapes of the walls, the narrow clayey passages with their constant humidity and dampness, suggest a special, womb-like refuge, which must have attracted men since the beginning of time.

The importance of the interior configuration of the cave—particularly the nature of the walls—should not be neglected. If we examine the walls of Lascaux, we are led to believe that the cave was chosen because of its smooth forms. Moreover, there are no stalagmites and it cannot be flooded: it is therefore quite hospitable, graphically speaking.

Length of Occupancy, Fauna

The age of the artworks in Lascaux has varied according to the methods used to determine it. Just after the discovery, several prehistorians—Abbé Breuil, Denis Peyrony and André Leroi-Gourhan—agreed that Lascaux was not typically Magdalenian, but might be older and belong to the Gravettian period. Since there was no organic matter on the walls, the paintings could not be dated by the carbon 14 method. At the end of the 1950's, the first datings through this method were made from charcoals found in the archeological floors: the cave was thought to have been occupied between 15,000 and 17,000 years ago. But in 2000, from samplings of a spear made out of reindeer antler found in the Shaft, scientists set the date at 18,600 years before the present. That is rather convincing, although it pushes back the dates previously put forth by a couple of thousand years: at the end of the Solutrean period and the very beginning of the Magdalenian, a time when the two cultures could have coexisted.

During the cold period in the southwest of Europe between 18,000 and 19,000 years before the present, the main food source of hunters was the great herds of hoofed herbivores: horse, aurochs, bison, red deer, ibex, Saiga antelope and reindeer. These animals also supplied weapons, protection from the cold and bad weather, clothing, ornaments. During that same period, we see the progressive extinction of the last giant herbivores: the mammoth, the Megaceros deer, the woolly rhinoceros, which were also the favorite prey of Paleolithic hunters. In the zones that could be excavated at Lascaux, excavations have revealed a predominance of reindeer, whereas this species is not represented on the walls. This absence could pose a problem for dating the paintings. If we assert that the painted animals yield information about the environment, then the artist lived in a temperate era; if we stick to food residues, we know that the reindeer lived during a cold period. The solution is probably between the two. In Lascaux we can indeed see the work of a society living in the midst of reindeer and using them for food, while maintaining a certain tradition—the tradition of horses and bulls.

Additionally, the fact that reindeer is what is mostly found in food residues gives us clues about the time of year when the cave was used. It must have been winter, the season when reindeer, the most abundant game and the easiest to kill, crossed the Vézère river. Finally, meat could easily be preserved by drying or stocking it in ice for three months during the winter.

Climate and Territory

Zones the hunters could inhabit during the cold glacial period were restricted to narrow strips along the coast, even though they were wider than they are now, since sea level was 120 meters lower than it is today. Geographical areas for the circulation of flocks and human groups were thus limited to confined territories along the edges of France and the Iberian Peninsula and up the Rhône valley from the Mediterranean coastline. The steep middle valleys of the coastal rivers and streams, which cut through the foothills of the mountainous zones, undoubtedly created sheltered zones that were much sought-after: they house most of the sites of this period, characterized by Solutrean and early Magdalenian cultures. The deposits at Laugerie-Haute, Jean-Blancs, Fourneau du Diable, Combe Saunière in Dordogne, Roc-de-Sers and Placard in Charente, Peyrugues in Lot are a few examples. The environment is characterized by hilly landscapes—wooded here and there, but with a cold, dry climate (sometimes humid, but rarely) typical of wide open steppes; it enables herds of hoofed animals to live there, and also species more specific to local microclimates. The northern limits of the territory marking the extension of Solutrean culture in France at this time are Mayenne, Vienne and Burgundy, with pockets in Charente, Aquitaine, in the foothills of the Pyrenees and the Massif Central and the lower parts of the west bank of the Rhône.

Structure of the Cave

The "receiving structure" is a concept defined by the prehistorian Henri Delporte for the study of habitat: we use it here to describe the nature of the mineral environment that supports the engraved and painted artworks. The limestone formation observed in Lascaux is the same as the one in the valley of Les Eyzies, but the limestone is special here. Indeed, it is far from the deep sea of Aquitaine where a mass of extremely hard limestone was deposited over a distance of two hundred meters. This was the case in Bordeaux, in Bergerac, and also at Les Eyzies. By the edge of that sea—that is, at Brive, Saintes, Cahors and Biarritz, where sea-shells, madrepores and corals have been found—limestone from the late Cretaceous Period became grittier and more granular instead, as at Montignac.

The walls do not have the same characteristics everywhere in the cave; the differences are more or less shared by the two galleries, to the right and to the left. In the left part, the Hall of Bulls and the Axial Passage, as well as the Shaft to the right, the limestone has been covered by pure, very hard and white, highly compact calcite of exceptional quality but difficult to work because of its hardness and irregular surface, which is made of "cauliflower" and tiny herring-bone (*spicular*) concretions. In the lower right-hand part, the limestone is not covered with calcite and has a softer surface. This distribution explains why the first part is unsuitable for engraving: work there can only be done by successive applications. The second part can also be painted, but it can be worked by removing matter as well—that is, engraving or sculpting. These physical characteristics of the wall-face did not go unnoticed by prehistoric men: they adapted to them and turned them to good account. They may even have appreciated the immaculate whiteness of the calcite in Lascaux and the possibilities this reflecting support gave them to use light colors—for example, yellow ochre or light red—and to obtain strong chromatic contrasts.

In Lascaux, it becomes clear that the whole iconographic composition of a cave depends on the geological structure of the wall and the topography of the spaces; so we speak of a "participating cave," a concept developed by André Leroi-Gourhan and then used by other prehistorians to understand the disposition of painted or engraved artworks—and also avoid making hasty interpretations.

Parietal Disposition

Describing the disposition of the artworks in Lascaux means giving shape and light to a series of spaces, of differences in level, of volumes distributed over a few dozen meters. More specifically, as the work of Norbert Aujoulat has shown, the space of the cave available for decoration is about 250 square meters, distributed over several autonomous spaces, each mineralogically distinct. On the north-south axis, from the entrance to the end of the Chamber of Felines, the total length does not go over 80 meters. The lowest zones are regularly invaded by carbonic gas, which can forbid access to the Shaft and the corridor leading to the Chamber of Felines, whereas the higher zones are usually free of gas. Giving an account of the whole means counting the juxtaposed and superimposed figures, enumerating the various artistic techniques, describing what strikes the eye and what escapes it, what keeps the observer at a distance and what can be deciphered on contact with the wall. It means giving an order—or unity?—to something that has none, connecting the two big bumpy axes of the cave with a few reassuring—and barbaric—words, thus giving it the appearance of a constructed, social body, both organic and spiritual. To place this group or that figure, we do use here, as in all caves, words from the vocabulary of architecture, anatomy and religion: the *Rotunda* (or *Hall of Bulls*), the *Axial Passage*[2] and

[2] "Axial Diverticulum" (*diverticule axial*) in French.

the *Chamber of Felines* enclose a zone of quiet meditation, the Apse and the Nave, which are separated from the world of light and darkness by the *Lateral Passage* and the *Shaft*. In the same way, a few elements of the bestiary are singled out for their obvious strangeness or expressiveness, by giving them elective names or qualifiers: the "Unicorn" (Abbé Breuil had named it the "Sphinx" in 1940), the "swimming red deer," the "Chinese horse," the "great black cow" characterize Lascaux as much as "the Shaft Scene."

Present access to the cave is the same as the one revealed by its discoverers. A second entrance time has rendered impassable, along the steep rock that used to mark the landscape on the side of the hill, may have existed further on to the right, to the side of the Shaft. But the disposition of the visual works accessible today in the first room lends a solemn, inaugural character to this space, like a curtain rising in the theater.

The Hall of Bulls

Hardly more than a few meters down, we look up and see one of the most ingenious compositions ever adapted to a mineral support. We don't know if this first decorated space was called the Rotunda because of its volume, actually more oval than round, or because of the 25 meter long animal frieze spread over the whole calcite surface and galloping towards a lateral confrontation, the color and movement of this dancing animal farandole blending perfectly with the color and movement of the wall.

A few figures, spectacular because of their size or nature, give this room a unique atmosphere—particularly the Unicorn, a composite creation, a genuine dream-like creature born from a painter's vision. It is stationed just at the left-hand entrance, along with five imposing aurochs, two on the left wall and three on the right. The fourth, on the right-hand wall, 5.5 meters long, is one of the largest depictions of an animal in prehistoric times. The highest lines are more than 3.5 meters above what was then the floor. These two animal friezes, composed of aurochs, horses, red deer, but also of a unicorn to the left and a bear to the right, mostly face the entrance to the Axial Passage, where they seem to enter or to stage a confrontation.

The Axial Passage

Facing the entrance, at the center of the Hall of Bulls, the Painted Gallery is integrated into the structure of this hall without disturbing the balance or movement of the great initial fresco. Narrow and winding on ground level, this cramped passage, about twenty meters long, widens toward the ceiling and narrows again mid-way. The abundant ornamentation appears high up, as the vertical walls are partly unsuitable (man-high) for the application of paint. From the entrance, in perspective, the black head of a red cow echoes the developed antlers of a red deer; four red cows arranged in mirror images follow the shape of part of the ceiling and the top section of the walls; the two dark, detached masses of a bull and a jumping cow lead, after many little horses, ibexes, and "Chinese horses"—all organized and grouped together—to the final narrowing meander-shaped cavity, marked on one side by figures of horses (one is called "upside down") and on the other, by a series of horses, red bison and abstract signs.

Every accessible zone has been decorated, particularly the cupola-shaped ceiling, where the white calcite has a very delicate crystallization that permits delicate painting technique—nuances of color (pale yellow, greenish yellow for the finest horses), with a thin black outline. The drawing is much more precise, light and realistic than it is on the lower levels, where the color had to be projected more violently and massively on the more irregular "cauliflower" surface.

The horses are organized in technical and stylistic groups: thus the more velvety outlines of the little horses at the end and the plumper horses on the right-hand wall contrast with the big yellow horses and the red and black cows of the ceiling at the entrance to the Gallery.

End of the Axial Passage and the Winding Passage

On one side to the left, several horses and the "hemione" (wild ass) follow each other up to the horse, which is depicted upside down, and seems to be surging up from the depths or falling into them. These figures show technical unity and are painted in the same tones. A very large, red branching sign is connected to them, while on the opposite side, three red figures and abstract signs go off into the narrow gallery. Less accessible, but nonetheless quite visible, since they are placed on the right-hand wall (the most regular one), the last bright red figures stand out in sharp contrast to the white wall; they are much more freely drawn than the other figures. The red bison, with its tail held up high and a black line on its back, seems a grotesque figure. The horse following it has zebra stripes along his back; his gaze, turned three-quarters towards us, which is unusual, evokes the gaze of the horse seen head-on at the other end of the cave, in the Chamber of Felines.

The Lateral Passage

As we return toward the Hall of Bulls, to the right, perpendicular to the Axial Passage, the Lateral Passage opens. This low space is a zone dividing two coherent wholes (Hall of Bulls – Axial Passage, and Apse – Nave) characterized by different rock supports and level-changes. From this point on, the bare limestone appears to be more friable and ill-suited for the preservation of paintings, but on the other hand more suitable for engraving. "It is interesting to wonder if this corridor, whose morphology is reminiscent of other sites like Les Combarelles, Le Gabillou (...), could not be more than a functional thoroughfare, but actually a coherent whole, to be analyzed independently from the other juxtaposed groups." (Denis Vialou, "*Le Passage et l'Abside*", in J. Allain *et al., Lascaux inconnu.*)

Two phases of execution may be detected in the Lateral Passage. The wall that was originally covered by burgeoning calcite, with an accented relief, functioned as a support for figures whose traces we can still see: animal legs and bellies at the level of the prehistoric floor. Large figures of horses and bison, comparable to those in the Hall of Bulls and the Axial Passage, must have completely decorated the low vault of this corridor.

Subsequently, chemical corrosion and the mechanical action of air circulating through the vault worked together to wear away the calcite and uncover the limestone underneath. Works of another style were then executed with the aid of other techniques adapted to this fine-grained support with a fairly tender surface. In the Passage, the Nave and the Apse, these techniques combine fine, precise, extremely realistic engraving with polychrome painting in numerous depictions of horses, bison, aurochs, and deer, organized in several distinct panels.

The Nave

At the end of the Passage a vast gallery opens up. It has a high vault (hence the old name "Nave,") characterized by the size of its engraved figures and by a few striking paintings on each side of the vault—the great black cow, the frieze of swimming red deer—clearly distinct from the others. It is also characterized by the presence of painted geometric outlines in checkerboard form, overlaid by an engraved line. The separate panels of the *Footprint* and the *Black Cow* are the most remarkable examples of this type of expression.

Low above the ground, under an overhanging vault, the panel called the *Footprint* is hard to reach. Over a stretch of two meters, framed by two black checkered signs, a herd of about ten horses stands out; a bison is superimposed over them at the far right end. The bodies of the main horses and the bison are marked by a series of lines: some of them are signs in the form of arrows.

The Panel of the Black Cow is only accessible through a narrow, horizontal cornice raised over the slanting floor. A black cow crowns a frieze of little horses of various colors maneuvering above a floor-line characterized by the brown clay at the bottom of the wall. The intentions of the authors of the frieze—to complete the work progressively—are particularly perceptible through the stages of the frieze's construction. Several palettes and stone lamps were found at the foot of the frieze, on the ledge of the entablature. The brightly colored checkerboards at the level of the hooves of the Black Cow, traditionally called "coats of arms," are unique in this form. They are painted in astonishing colors like carmine and purplish pink.

Directly opposite the panel of the Black Cow, at the same level—that is, over the observer's head—a frieze of five red deer heads looking upwards is arranged above the fictitious line formed on the opposite side, but here by the calcite coming up the wall. The first four heads are drawn with a black line, but the last one is drawn with brown clay.

When we go straight towards the end of the Nave, while the narrowing space seems to have no exit, a couple of bison, back to back, at the bottom of the left-hand wall, make up the last painting of this part of the cave. They are arranged in the only visible free space in this zone of the cavity; the symmetrical effect of the composition, cleverly exploited, prevents us from seeing this as a simple group.

The Chamber of Felines

The adjacent passage is only accessible by crawling. Its exploration reveals the artworks most removed from the entrance to the cave. Access is difficult, as one must cross a shaft that is now always filled with carbonic gas. Perhaps because of the danger, this sector has rarely been visited; otherwise the works would have been erased by the constant traffic. If the numerous engravings are still quite visible, the paintings, on the other hand, show definite erosion. Among the depictions of bison, ibex, of many horses and engraved and painted signs, three silhouettes stand out, with clumsily drawn feline heads—hence the name of the group.

In the whole zone we are describing, the panels appear thematically distinct and topographically disconnected. This double characteristic is more obvious here than in the other spaces of the cave; there do not seem to be graphic elements that might link the Footprint, the Black Cow, the two bison drawn back to back, the red deer and the Chamber of Felines.

The Apse

Tracing our steps back from the Chamber of Felines to the exit from the Passage, we can access a very special part of the cave on our left, called the Apse because of its shape. It has a special status, as much for its topographical position—a nucleus branching into the galleries of the Passage, the Nave and the anfractuous Shaft—as for the function of its walls: the lower parts reveal a palimpsest of paintings and engravings. The upper part could only have been decorated by an ingenious arrangement of masts used for scaffolding.

The Shaft

The orifice is several meters deep. Half way up, a narrow landing, only accessible to the people of Lascaux by means of ropes;

it nonetheless gave them a rather precarious foothold facing a wall receptive to paint. The representations figuring here stand out without any superimposition: a rhinoceros on one side, a bird-headed man lying between a disemboweled bison and a stick crowned by a bird's head are among the most famous rock art paintings in the world.

Through chemical analysis of the materials used in the painting, we now know that the rhinoceros and the series of dots following it were not painted at the same time as the other elements. Still, we cannot specify the order in which they were painted. This discovery is a reminder that different compositions in the cave were painted at different times, and certain panels were completed progressively.

In a sense, the "Shaft Scene" matches the scene of the two back-to-back bison at the very end of the Nave. These two works were painted directly with a brush, without making a sketch, with a mastery reminiscent of the classical art of Chinese painting and a precision of outline that calls for a similarly precise narrative. Nothing hinders the gaze, neither the superimposition nor the juxtaposition of other figures. In both cases, the wall seems to have been chosen for the same reasons: it is covered by golden-yellow calcite. An incomplete horse, technically similar, stands alone facing the scene.

The Archeological Materials

Many objects have been found scattered all over the ground of the cave. Flint tools (burins, scrapers) were used for engraving, cutting and sculpting; they were often left on the flat ledges of a wall, perhaps for future use. As for lighting, Lascaux has yielded an exceptional number of lamps, whether intact or in fragments; occasionally, some of the particularly fine ones are difficult to distinguish

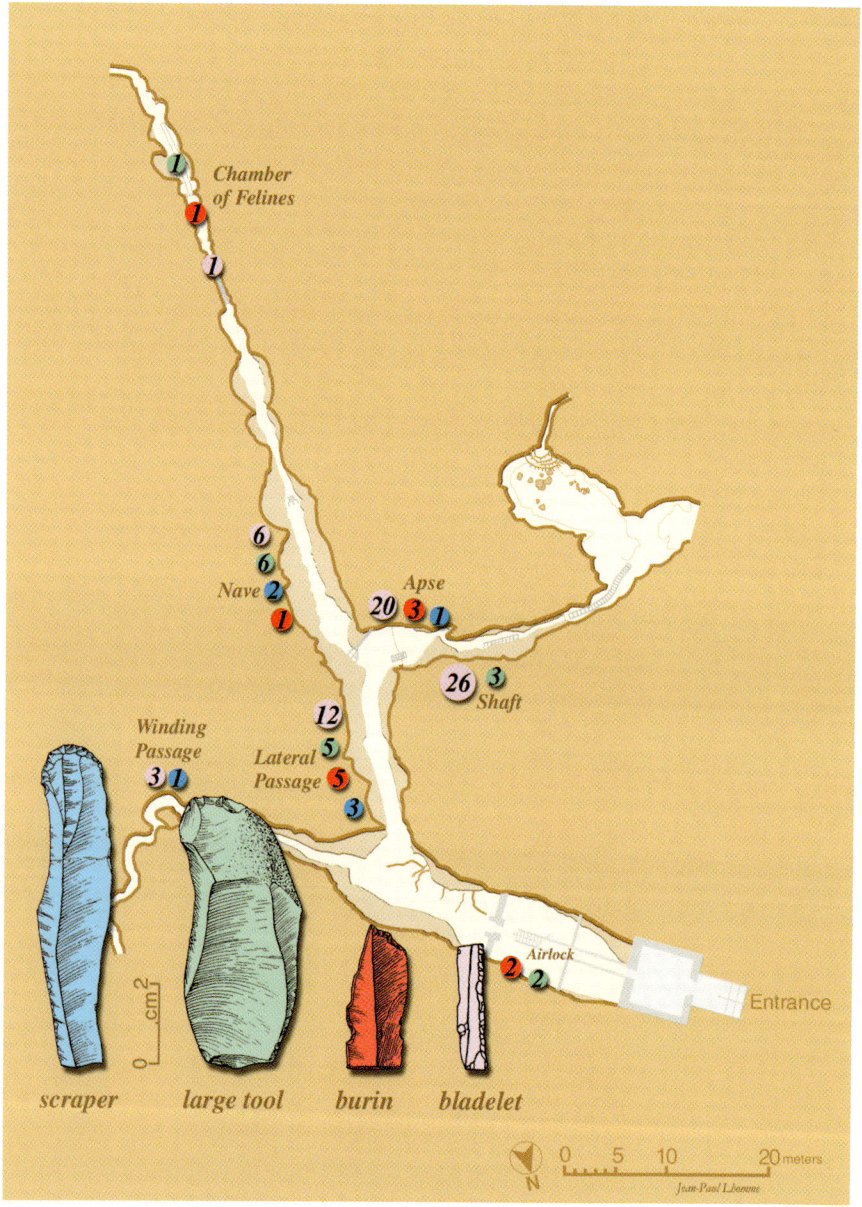

Chamber
of Felines
1
1
1
6
6
Nave
2
1
Apse
20
3
1
26
3
Shaft
12
5
Lateral
Passage
5
3
Winding
Passage
3
1
Airlock
2
2
Entrance
0
cm
2
scraper
large tool
burin
bladelet
0
5
10
20 meters
N
Jean-Paul Lhomme

FLINT TOOLS

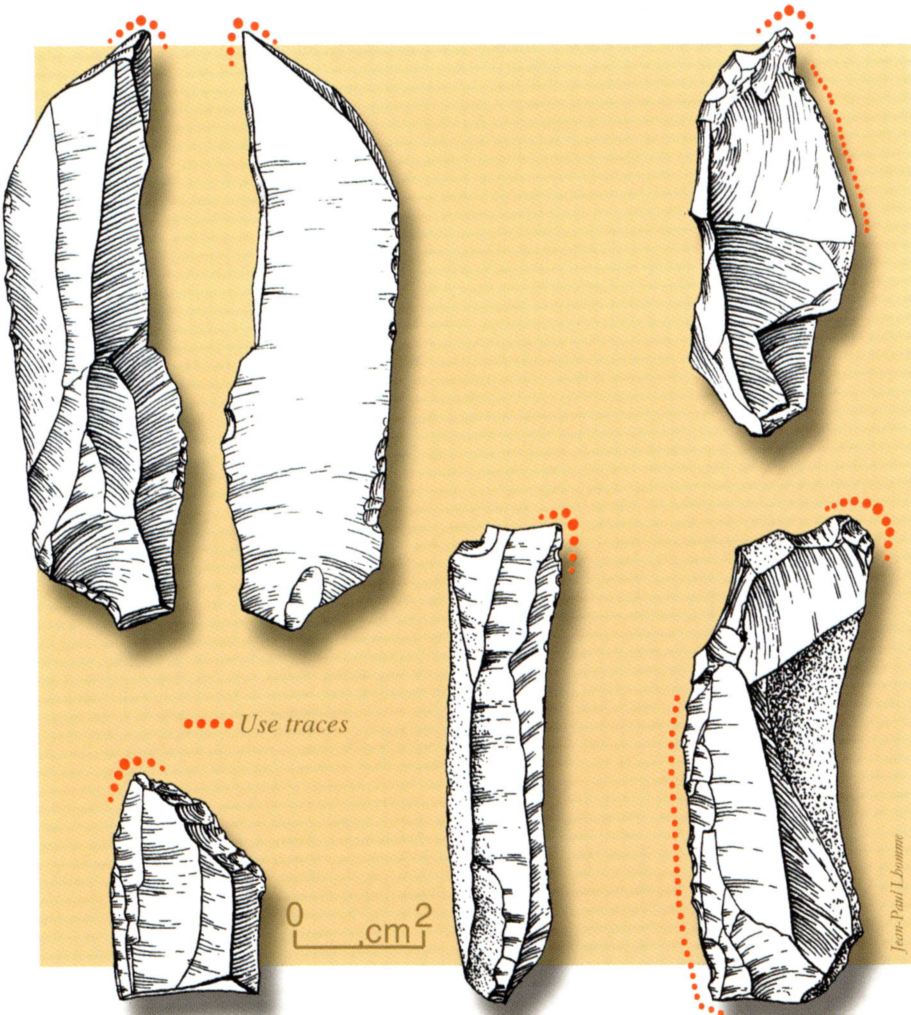

Engraving tools

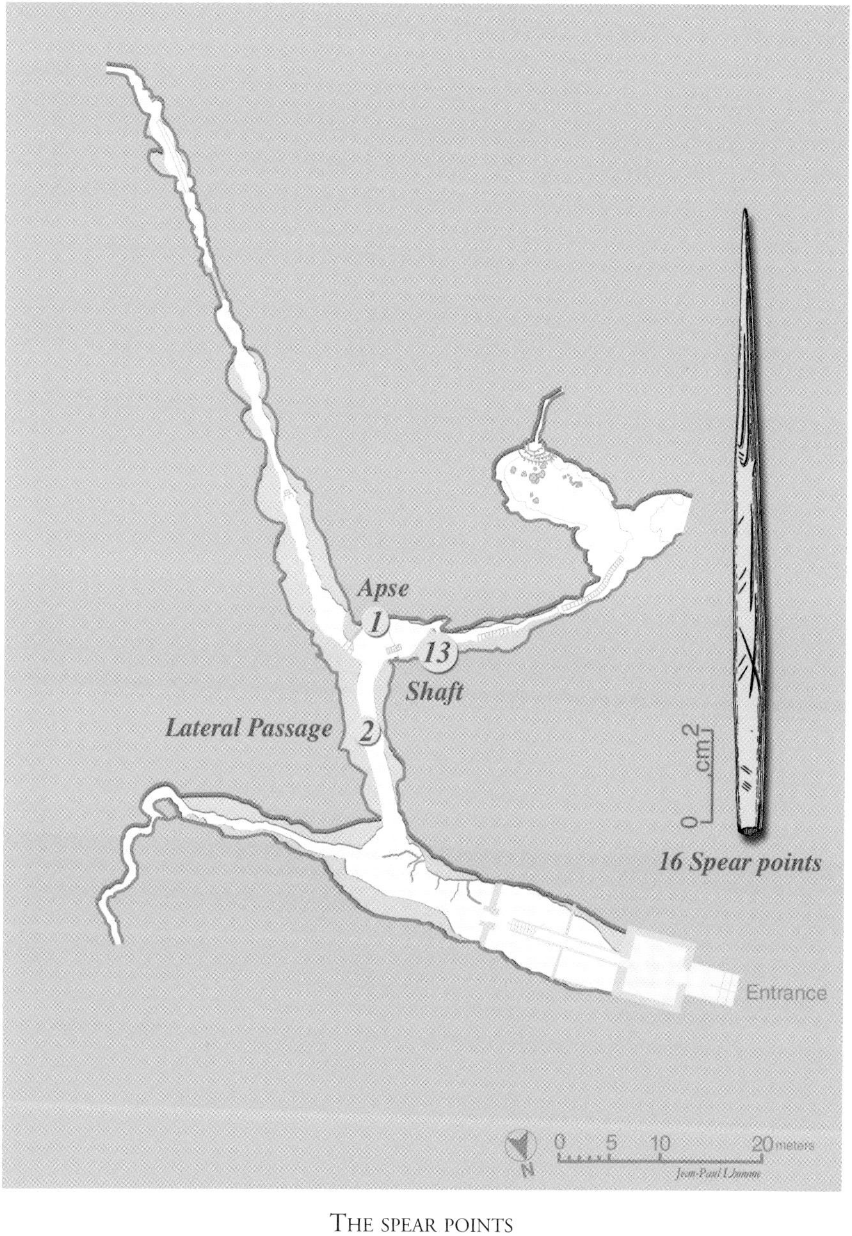

THE SPEAR POINTS

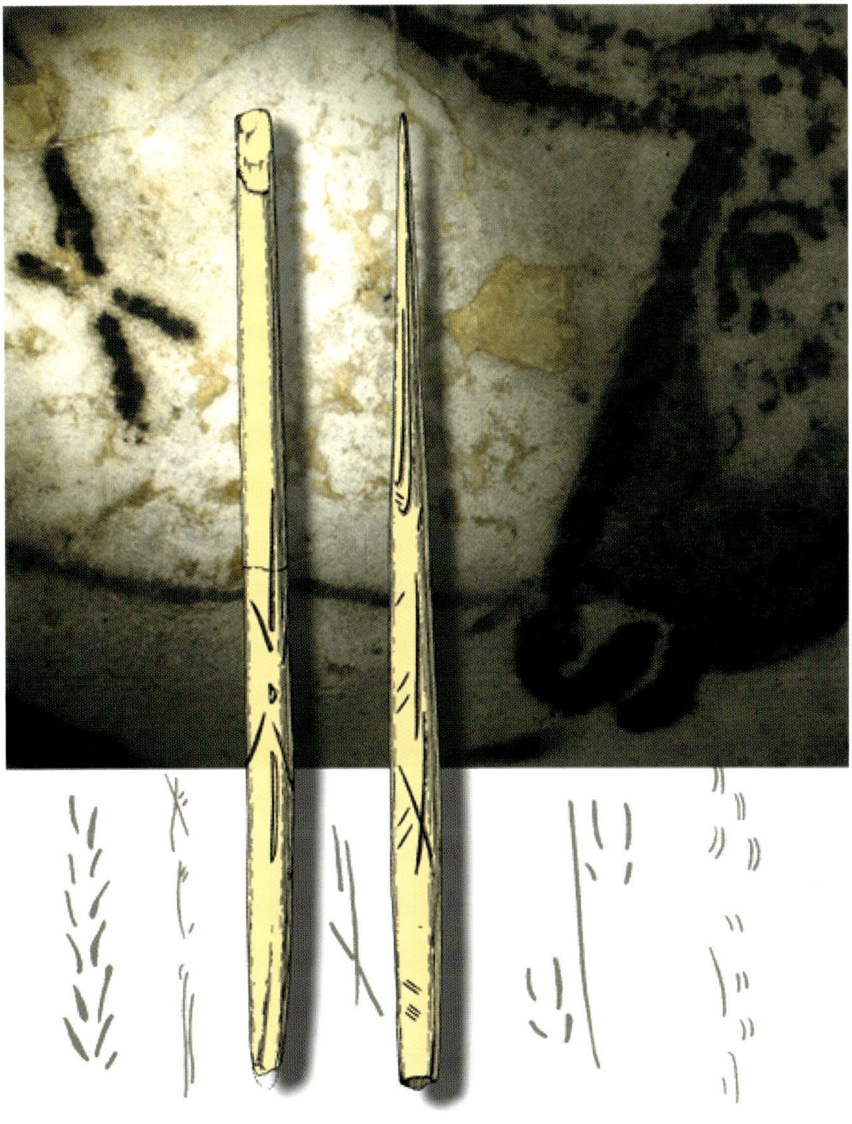

Spear point decorations

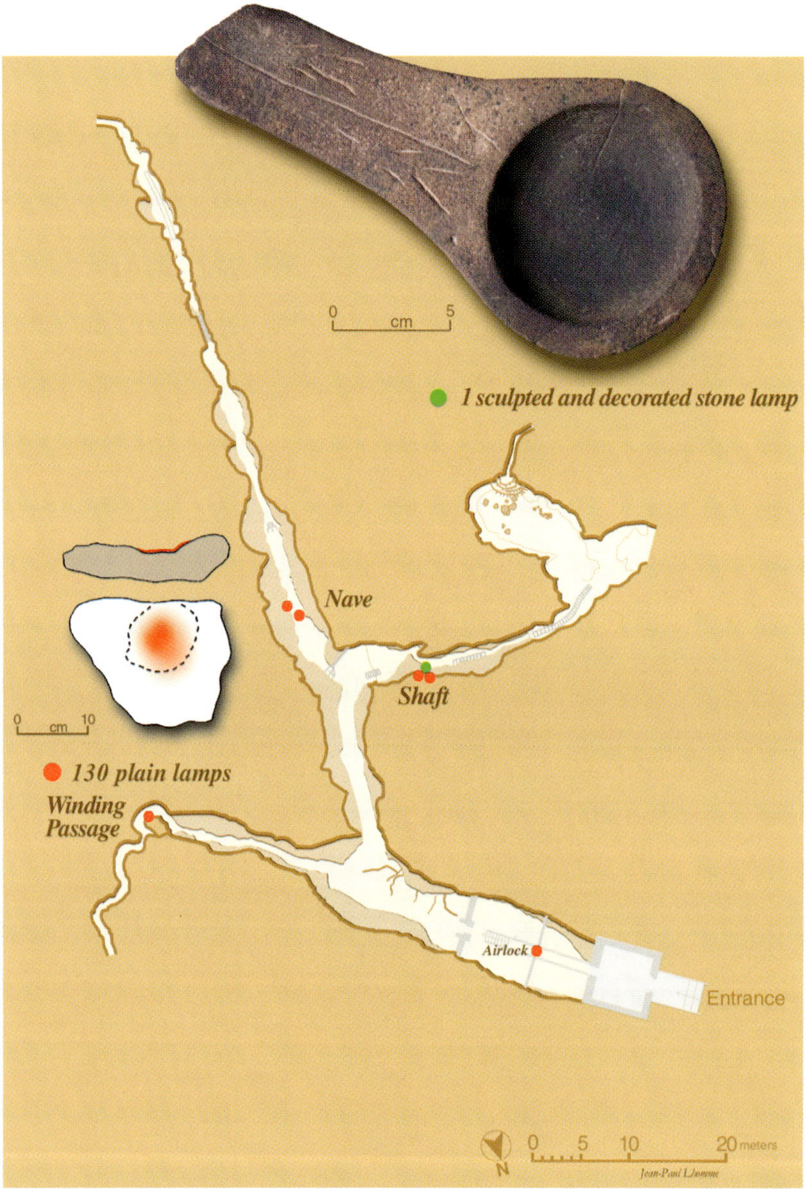

THE LIGHTING

in shape from palettes. The lighting system of the cave has turned out to be extremely complete. Lamps abandoned along some of the walls may have enabled various panels to be completely illuminated. There is no known analogous example. The palettes, hollowed out of stone, still contained color when they were discovered. Receptacles may have been necessary to paint the great bulls; for iron oxide, containers (skins, plants) were probably needed to mix water and pigment. There is no trace of the grinders they used, but the ochre might have been brought into the cave in powder form before onsite preparation. The palettes might also have been used to crush oxide fragments or to mix ochre. Good "pencils" in various materials (iron oxide and manganese oxide) have also been found.

Among the bones collected, there were reindeer bones, both as food residues and material used to make weapons for hunting, projectile or spear-points, also sculpted in ivory. The geometric decoration of the spears is the same as some of the motifs found on the walls. These objects were concentrated in the Apse, particularly at the bottom of the Shaft where Abbé Glory exhumed a very fine lamp in pink sandstone, whose handle has the same signs as the spears. This fact can be explained by the heavy traffic within this perimeter adjoining the Shaft: these objects, which may have a votive character, could have slipped in or been thrown in. In any case, there is a kind of opposition between the accumulation of these deposits near the Shaft and the isolated, hidden work at its end.

The Range of Techniques

All the techniques of the era were used: paint was thrown on or laid on, used in more or less liquid form, sometimes pasty; the outlines were prepared by "pencilling" them in black, or, more frequently, sketched out in red, with a brush. Red and black paint were supplied by the surrounding environment, with iron oxide (yellow ochre or natural red, sometimes heated to make it darker or brighter) and manganese oxide, which is highly abundant in the region. Natural yellow ochre is rarely used in other caves, perhaps because the natural color of their walls is yellow. But in Lascaux, the calcite-covered walls are white, so it was possible to work the whole range of light shades: pale yellow, pale gray, light red and pink. This is why it is only in Lascaux, and to a lesser extent in Altamira, that we can see real polychromatic painting, that is, a mixture of shades on the same figure and not superimposed layers of paint. Thus the artists were able to apply black mixed with yellow or gray, red mixed with black, yellow with red.

Ochre in Lascaux was used in powdery form. Men discovered, as early as 25,000 to 30,000 years before us, that they could turn natural orange-yellow pigment to red by heating it in fireplaces over 300° C. and as high as 600° C. With the exception of a coat of arms at the foot of the Black Cow, they do not seem to have used white or pearly pink (observed in archeological sites contemporary to Lascaux) obtained from a clay containing kaolin, but these paints may have been destroyed. Nor is there any trace of charcoal for the color black, since Lascaux is in the geographic and cultural area where manganese is used. However, chemical analysis has proved that small quantities of burned crushed bone were often combined with this basic pigment. This addition may have been dictated by technical considerations, or by the rules of a tradition or the demands of some religious cult. In any case, the black pigment was in a sufficiently viscous state to be blown on or applied by brush or stamp.

The Lascaux artists often relied on the technique of stamping. The painters worked with stamps made out of fur or plants, tightly bound; we can see clear traces of small, very round stamps, three to
 four centimeters long, dipped in the paint-pot and applied to the

wall. The stamp could also be used as a brush, rubbed sideways. As the calcite-covered wall is extremely uneven, a tool of fur hairs or plant fiber, 2-3 centimeters thick, enabled the artists to thoroughly impregnate the support, but they had to apply hundreds of these little stamps to make the dotted outlines of the great black bulls. Most of the paint was then laid on with larger stamps or by airbrush, using an instrument (cut reed, bamboo), or blown directly out of the mouth. The latter technique can be performed very simply by spitting out the liquid paint held in the mouth near the wall, or by mixing powdered pigment and water in the mouth, which avoids using bulky receptacles. This is the "spitting" technique.

The artists used the brush and the stamp to obtain clear outlines, and airbrushing to cover the surfaces. To prevent the blown paint from overflowing and to reduce blurring, they used their hands, their arms or cutouts of organic materials (skin, leather, and bark) as stencils. These techniques of stamping and airbrushing were particularly adapted to the mineral support: as the surface of the wall has a cauliflower texture 1 to 2.5 centimeters thick, they had to apply or project a large quantity of paint, whether pasty (stamped) or liquid (blown) and use safe-edges to stay inside the outlines.

The examination of artistic techniques includes the problem of the accessibility of the wall. The artists either had to work at arm's length or pressed up against the wall. Irregular lines have been found, produced with a brush or a stamp probably attached to the end of a stick and held at arm's length 1.5 meters over the artist's head. In places where the paint was blown out, the mouth had to be placed about 30 centimeters from the wall. Thus the painter had to have direct access to the wall through little flat areas, small steps he could stand on; or else he worked with an assistant, if only for the lighting—a little team to install the artworks. This installation required guiding marks, although we rarely find traces

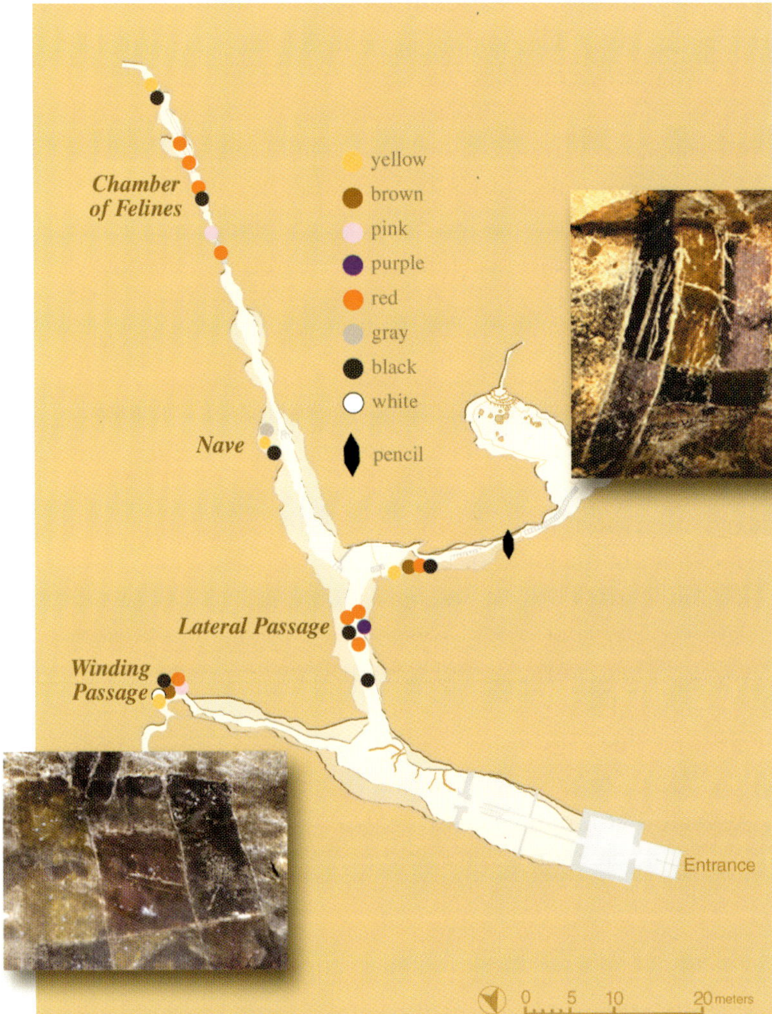
Chamber of Felines
Nave
Lateral Passage
Winding Passage
Entrance
yellow
brown
pink
purple
red
gray
black
white
pencil
N
0 5 10 20 meters
Jean-Paul Lhomme

PAINTS

of them. They are usually an outline—an animal's back or parts of its head and extremities: this is how we can see that some outlines had been placed elsewhere.

Certain parts of arched ceilings could have been painted with scaffolding; but these parts have remained intact, which makes this hypothesis doubtful. Besides, there are no archeological traces of this set-up. The painters may occasionally have used a very simple ladder, to reach the dome of the Apse for example, but in general one or two assistants were enough to maintain at a given height the feet or back of the man who was working without any other comfortable support. Anywhere that the wall is accessible, the painter could climb up and get a good foothold, if necessary by using a branch or two so as not to slip. With two or three men against the wall in the Hall of Bulls, mastering the space was not all that hard. Making the great Black Cow of the Nave was the riskiest situation: the artist worked out of balance on a small lip 60 cm wide, with the wall slanting back towards him; even in that case, getting support from another person may have been sufficient. In the Axial Passage, for certain high points, the painter could stand with his legs spread apart between the two walls. Finally, if we put ourselves in the artist's place and take his viewpoint, we can see that the interference of beams and platforms between his eye and such complex works could have been harmful to their production.

The Artist's Gaze and the Viewer's Eye

The set of conditions for executing these artworks includes the problem of the gaze—the master artist's and those who look at the works. The location of the figures was chosen according to a

Access to the walls

Access to the walls

great many criteria: form and texture of the walls, accessibility, lighting, etc. At the same time, the spectator's viewpoint was taken into consideration. One may say that there is a back-and-forth movement between the artist who tried to install his work and the painter, as he climbed back down again, saw what it looked like, thought about how the community might view it. This back-and-forth movement of the same gaze, or perhaps of a community of gazes, was taken into account.

On the contrary, in other caves or certain parts of Lascaux itself, the painter ignored the outside gaze, and some works—hidden, inaccessible—were not made to be seen. This is true of the artworks in the Shaft and the Chamber of Felines, where access could be dangerous. Only one person could work in the Shaft; the bison and the man are above the artist's eye and one must be at the bottom to see the work from the spot where it was painted. At the end of the Axial Passage, two horses and a bison painted in bright red monochromes contrast, by their rather crude execution, with what has been called "the Upside-down Horse" just opposite them. These works were not intended to be viewed in the same way as the one in the Shaft or the two back-to-back bison.

The gaze of the people of Lascaux on the ornamentation of the cave was subjected to lighting, diffused by stone lamps or torches with two characteristics that made them different from our modern lighting: their lower intensity defines a smaller field and their instability sets the shadows in motion and animates the light. It is in the nature of Paleolithic light to be three-dimensional. In other words, only a part of the Rotunda's fresco, for example, was visible for someone coming into the cave, unless dozens of lamps were installed and held aloft. Thus the "viewer" would only discover the bulls successively, like figures in a narrative. The painter who had conceived the arrangement was the only one to have a view of the whole—at least in his mind. Contrary to what will happen from the Renaissance on with paintings executed on an easel, none of the Paleolithic painters could immediately have the spectator's vantage point as they worked.

> The semi-circle of the Lascaux Rotunda incited the artist to execute vast circular friezes of animals that seemed to trot across a fictitious ground formed by a rocky, horizontal base, giving relief to the wall. They were intended to be seen by a group of worshippers placed in the center of the room or used as a backdrop for activities taking place at this spot. In the same way, the long, horizontal bands of the Axial Passage, the Lateral Passage and the Nave of the same cave explain the presence of long lines of animals—among them, the group of "swimming red deer" with their heads raised; the surface of the water is suggested by the rocky ledge. In contrast, the dome of the Apse is covered by a swirling tangle of engravings. (Michel Lorblanchet, *Les Grottes ornées.*)

In the Hall of Bulls, the big bulls are placed where they can be clearly seen and appreciated. The lower part of the walls, which is black, was not suitable for painting, and neither was the dark, concave middle part, but the ceilings were accessible. The largest figures are arranged so as to be perfectly legible, with an obvious attention to staging. The viewpoint systematically adopted places them above the observer's head, producing an effect of overhanging circularity. We find the same device at Altamira, Pech-Merle and Font-de-Gaume, where the gaze rises over the vanishing line.

> To experience this Quaternary western fully, the visitor should stand at the entrance to the passage under the hindquarters of the 5,50 meter long aurochs whose powerful arrowed head expresses healthy exhilaration.

> By a curious effect of perspective due to the slant and the increasing curve of the rocky wall, you can see the tumultuous horde of all the animals gathered around the first two bulls (...)
> We do not know if the artists had intended this kinematic effect, but we must give credit to the intuitive genius of the various authors who exploited the underground setting to animate this spectacular hunting scene so stunningly.
> (André Glory, *Lascaux : Versailles de la préhistoire,* Imprimerie Leymarie, Périgueux, 1978.)

Artworks at eye-level (the most numerous) were distinguished from works that dominate the viewers by their size or position as early as the Paleolithic, a distinction rediscovered at the height of the Renaissance by Michelangelo, at a time when high-placed frescoes were especially common. In both cases, the work was made to be seen in the air, floating, rather ethereally, even seen as if in a three-quarters low angle shot, in the position where viewers could see angels' backsides or the insides of togas on the ceilings of churches and palaces. In Lascaux we find a similar choice, with the cows seen from underneath, the red deer that have been called "swimming", the horses "floating": all are in fact positioned that way, above our line of sight.

At the time the cave was occupied, everything in the Lateral Passage was decorated, and men would move along under a painted vault, almost on their hands and knees, again more or less as they did in Font-de-Gaume. They would thus be moving through a narrow passage, a womb-like universe, forced to bow down under the artworks. Symbolically this is not without meaning. This kind of disposition is not unique to Lascaux, and the regularity of the morphologies of decorated caves is remarkable. Many caves are complex, branching, with endless corridors; on the contrary, Lascaux has the peculiarity of being small—it provides nice volumes over its eighty meters—and fairly well lit.

Today as yesterday, many smaller works are less easy to see. We must also mention the incomplete works—heads, red deer antlers, isolated legs—and an impressive number of geometric signs inscribed in the slightest anfractuosities and cracks, particularly in the Apse:

> Over a space of several square meters, there is not one inch of space free of engraved lines, scrapes, stripes, or colors. The walls of the Apse are as fully covered as some engraved stones, such as those of La Marche; no other wall, and thus of course no other underground room, even the "sanctuary of Les Trois Frères," can be compared to it. (...)
> (Denis Vialou, *Le Passage et l'Abside* in J. Allain et al., *Lascaux inconnu.*)

Cultural Stability

It is surprising that this sanctuary, which houses such special works, should have remained intact for more than ten thousand years without alteration, or accumulation of artworks, or any perceptible palimpsest. The large quantity of engravings concentrated in the Apse is proof of intense activity, and may indicate that occupancy in this part of the cave was independent from the occupancy marked by the great monumental paintings. We can theorize that the Apse is the ancient sanctuary, where engraving dominates, and the painted parts were occupied afterwards; that would explain why they remained intact.

We have few examples of pre-existing works being altered, due to the great stability of Paleolithic cultures, which were slow to change: it seems that for three or four thousand years nothing changed, neither traditions nor the structures of myths. Such respect for the artworks only surprises us because it has become foreign to modern man. For over two thousand years now, we have seen one civilization replace another and erase its culture; we also have forgotten the oral transmission of mythical memory, as written communication took over.

This respect for the paintings should not be understood as a cultural attitude to something perceived as a "work of art," but as respect for the memory of living beings—for the representation of life—which is not to be destroyed. A very strong taboo probably prevented anyone from touching the animal figures, symbols of living beings. We can see this quite clearly in La Mouthe Cave at Les Eyzies: each phase of occupancy (Gravettian or Perigordian, Solutrean and then Magdalenian) is represented in distinct spaces.

As a general rule, in Lascaux as elsewhere, there was neither destruction nor appropriation. The superimpositions always work by respecting the logic of the preceding layer and do not alter the composition of the whole. In the Hall of Bulls, we can see superimpositions: to the left, after the Unicorn, we have a group of intertwining shapes; the outlines of a bull stop to incorporate part of a large horse and part of a small one. A bit further, on the other hand, we can see large red bulls superimposed on black pre-existing works, but by applying red to black, the artist was careful to let us see through the two figures, and not to erase the older image. In the Axial Passage, on the left-hand side, we find the opposite: the great black bull partially obliterates two red cows, and more particularly, seems to precede four pale yellow bull heads, barely visible on the upper outline of the animal, contrasting with the white wall.

14

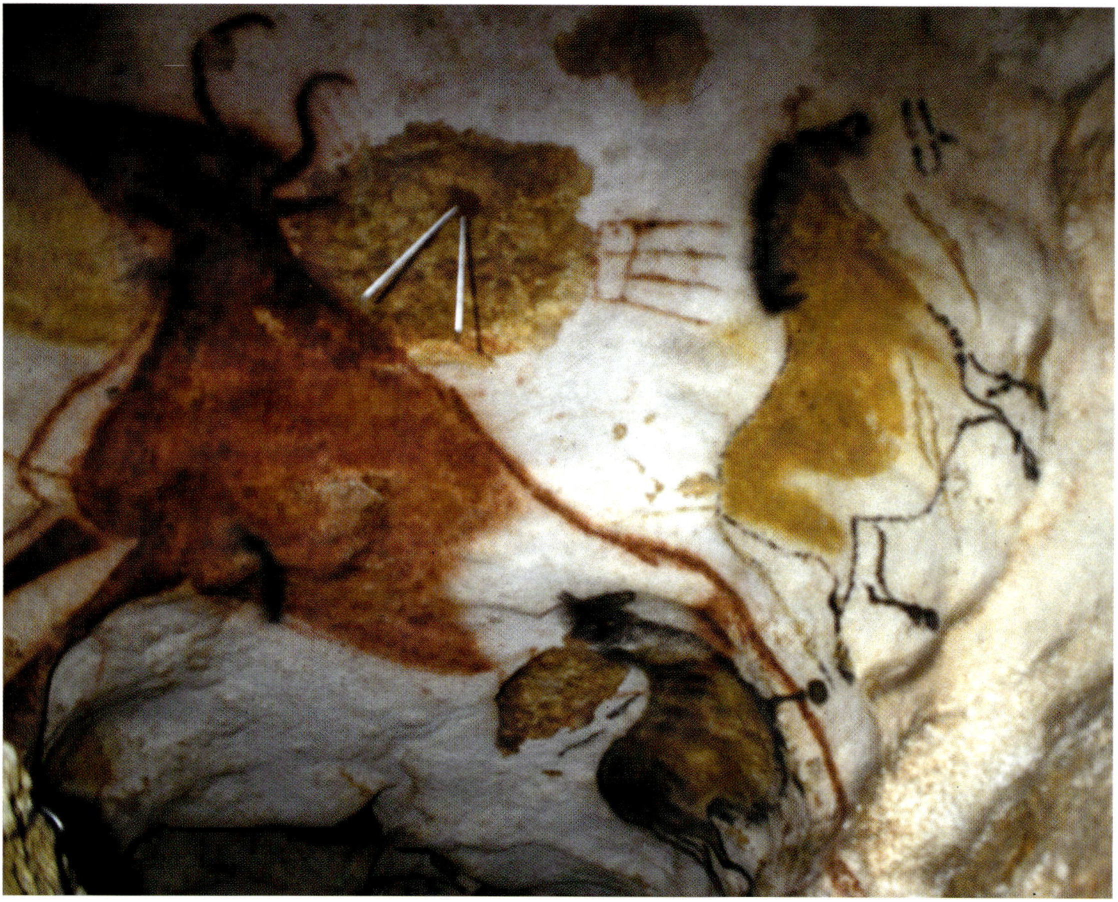

15

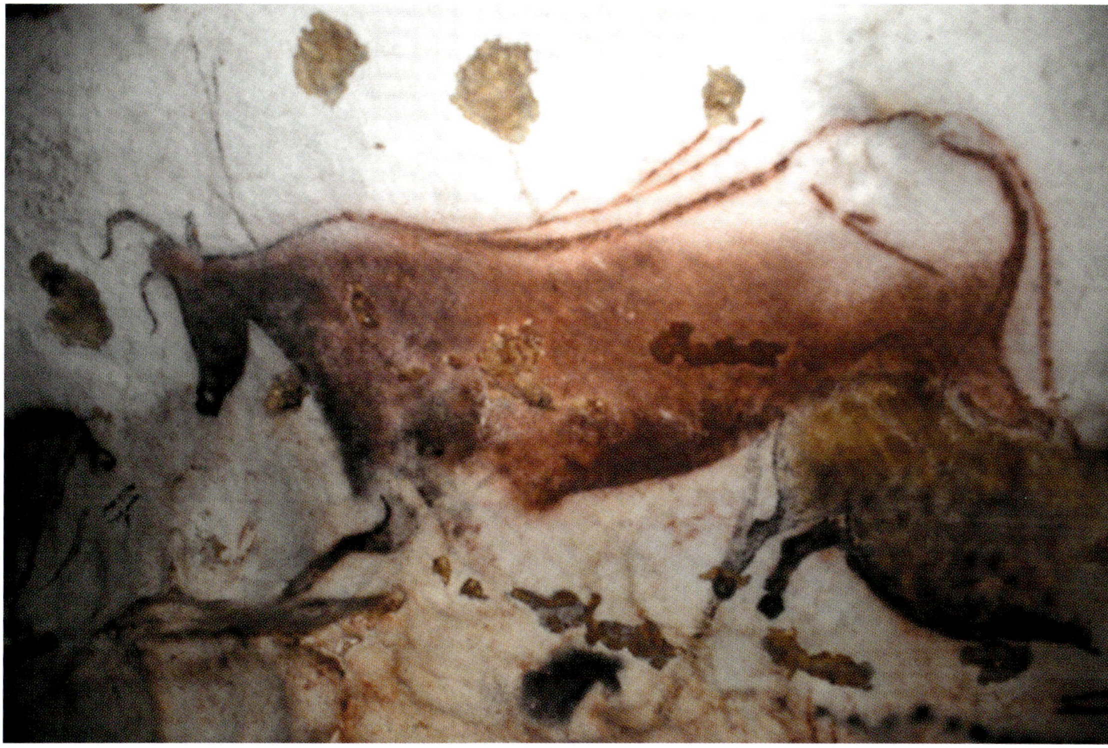

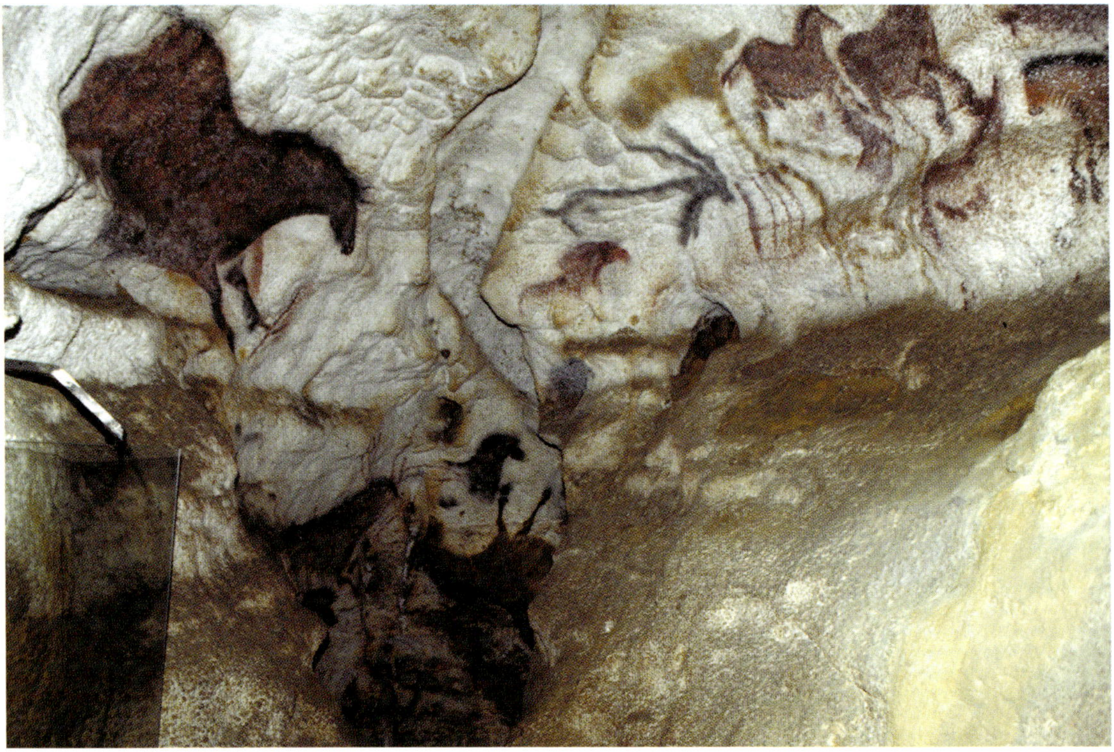

17

24

25

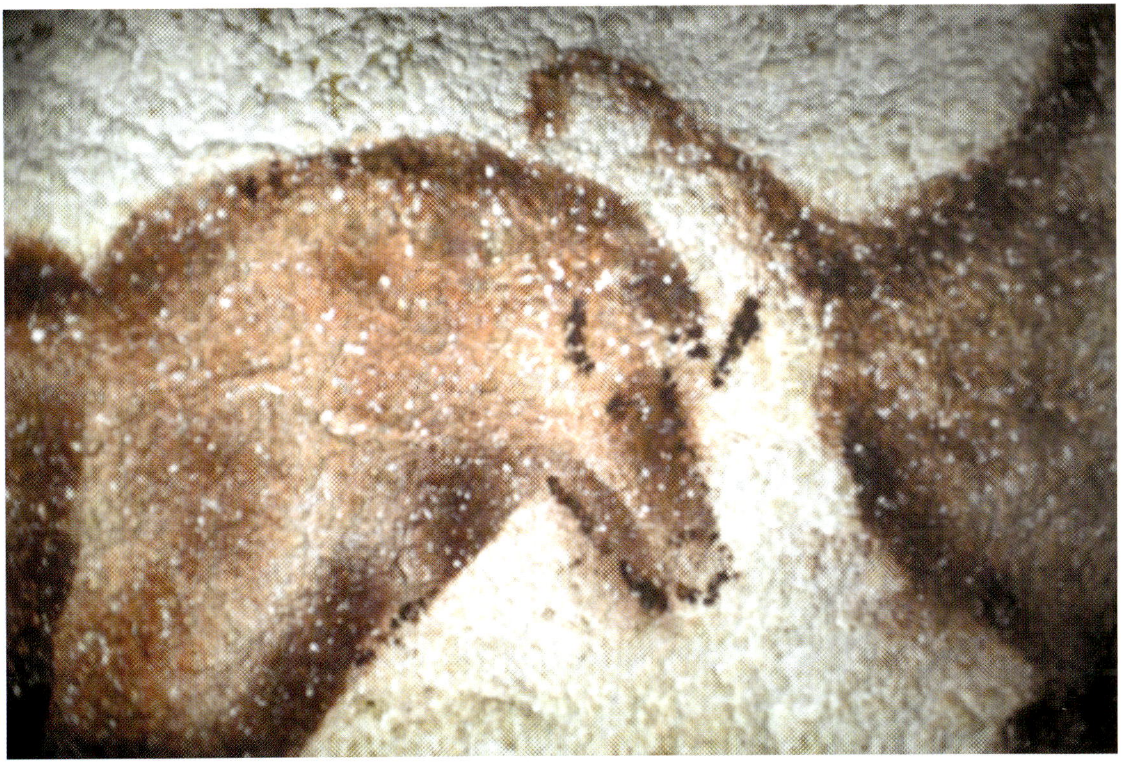

Axial Passage

Red deer's forequarters with signs at the entrance to the Painted Gallery (14.)
Horses and cows at the entrance arch (15, 16.)

Overall view of the end of the Axial Passage and the right wall (17.)
Detail of the right wall with ibexes symmetrically grouped around a checkered sign; these signs are unique to Lascaux (18.)

Left wall of the Axial Passage: big black bull obliterating two red cows drawn first. Under the head of the big black bull, the silhouette of a horse in yellow ochre is emphasized by a superimposed branching sign (19.)
Thorns in yellow ochre are visible over the neck-line of the big black bull (20.)
In front of the big brown horse located after the big black bull, a red cross-shaped sign (21.)

End of the Axial Passage, left wall: spit-painted horse; its nostrils, mouth and tail are emphasized by a black line drawn with a brush. A series of red dots and a large, red branching sign are superimposed over it (22.)
Detail of the head and neck of the preceding horse (23.) The last horse of the left wall is upside-down and seems to surge up from the terminal passage (24.)

Right wall of the terminal winding passage of the Axial Passage: the last two red animals (bison and horse), painted at the level of the original floor, were hard to reach at the time (25.)
Detail of the head of the last red horse in the winding passage of the Axial Passage (26.)

THE WORK OF TIME AND MEMORY

Neglected Engravings

As soon as you enter the Lascaux Cave, you see the paintings in the Hall of Bulls, and they are enormous. The many engravings do not occupy the same places as the paintings; they are concentrated in the Apse, and in a different way, present along the whole length of the Chamber of Felines. Men spent hours scraping the hard wall of the Apse to trace out shapes, prolong or cover lines that were already there, or just carve out certain lines, and the slightest fissures are striped. The engravings themselves are extremely varied: figurative drawings coexist with geometric tracings that are more or less expressive, completed animals can be seen next to incomplete ones, and next to signs. Right next to the Apse, the ceiling of the Nave has been striped by hitting it hard with sticks, sharp instruments or spear points. These stripes may recall the back-to-back bison or the animals of the Footprint, striated with lines and clearly depicted arrows.

And yet the interpretation of this extraordinary profusion of lines has been neglected compared to the paintings. We may remember that in the study of rock art, paintings were generally valorized far more than engravings from the very start. In Altamira, for example, where the engravings were discovered after the paintings, it took a long time for the link between the two to be discussed. In Lascaux, the diagrams made by Abbé André Glory between 1952 and 1963 were only partially published, with a description by Denis Vialou (in *Le Passage et l'Abside, op. cit.*) The lack of studies has caused the public to definitely favor paintings over engravings in its appropriation of the place, even when creating the replica of Lascaux, which only shows the parts of the cave with no engravings. Several reasons may explain why the engravings have been partly or totally "forgotten."

For one thing, we should not forget that in our time, outside of rock art, the market value for painting is higher than for engraving; this fact probably influences our perception of the works. But the problem of techniques of restitution has a role to play here, too: in our society, color is much more attractive than black and white lines, which seem to flatten everything out. Moreover, the black line on a white background, historically linked to the invention of the printing press, does not render rock art at all: it takes a white line on a black background to evoke Paleolithic engraving through pictures. This is completely contrary to our habits, so with few exceptions, only specialized publications give a real idea of the drawings.

How, then, are we to see and read the engravings that are so unfamiliar to our eyes? Thanks to the drawings available today, we can see animal figures, completed or not, among those thousands of lines. As in the paintings, the majority of them are horses, which suggests the idea of a strong link between the two activities. But painting makes outlines stand out and makes the animal figures visible to every viewer, whereas the engravings have the peculiarity of being intertwined, covering each other, and the superimposition of lines makes it impossible to distinguish the shapes clearly in the cave.

Outside of a few painted drawings and some rare, deeply carved silhouettes, nothing is immediately visible or readable, and never completely from just one viewpoint, with stable

> lighting: the figures turn on the rocky volumes, become entwined and mix together, forming complex decorative sequences. (Denis Vialou, *Le Passage et l'Abside* in *op. cit.*)

At the time of Lascaux, the informed viewer could recognize a little horse here, an ibex there, etc.; accompanied by the man who had carved the wall, he would have seen the animals as they were pointed out to him. But one may also think that the engravings did not have the same status as the paintings and were not meant to be looked at; this hypothesis cannot really be neglected. As a place that saw heavy traffic, the Apse was a space where every individual could establish a physical relationship with the parietal support, leave a trace—simple lines or a drawing related to the themes of the paintings. Or just touch it: repeated touching above the Shaft has polished the wall, just as in historic times the hands of worshippers polished the statues of saints.

From another point of view, we may say that for someone coming into the Apse, the engraved work seemed to be another kind of expression from the paintings nearby; it could be decoded, read, and enriched, depending on the memory and skill of the viewer. It was there as a surface for collective memory, with multiple meanings; as opposed to the painted panels, its characteristic was not to present precise shapes. It did not lend itself to interpretation or the building of a narrative. Non-linear, it served as a canvas on which the imagination of the people of Lascaux could feed.

Finally, the engraved sector of the Apse, which is also a womb-shaped alcove, gives access to the Shaft and contrasts with it; here everyone has left a trace, there, nothing has been touched: objects were thrown into the Shaft (lamps, tools, spears), but the painted work remained immaculate. The relationship between the Apse (an engraved surface) and the Shaft (a hole with figures) in

Lascaux can be compared to similar structures elsewhere. In Rouffignac Cave (Dordogne), the Great Painted Ceiling is there above a hole a few meters deep which has two bison and a man's face drawn on it; in the Trois-Frères Cave (Ariège), a wall with figures stands over a gulf that has a jumble of lines in it. Inside that jumble, Abbé Breuil singled out a figure he called a "sorcerer."

Animals and Man

Hundreds of animal representations, painted or engraved, whole or barely sketched silhouettes, easily recognizable or mixing several species, cover the walls of Lascaux. When they are counted and classified, horses are the most numerous, along with red deer, far more than aurochs, cows, bison, ibex, felines, rhinoceros—but quantity is not the only important element here. In fact, no depiction of reindeer can be found in the cave, whereas this animal was the favorite game of the people of Lascaux: food leavings found on site bear witness, as 88% of them are bone fragments of reindeer. We may also note the absence of images of animals—whether hunted or not—which were certainly present in the daily life of the Paleolithics: wolves, hyenas, birds of prey, hares, insects. Moreover, at the entrance to the Hall of Bulls there is a painted hybrid animal, which has been called "the Unicorn."

The relationship of man to animal was that of the hunter to his prey, but what the works in Lascaux teach us goes far beyond the quest for food through magical techniques.

> The certainty of the existence of a mythical animal [the Unicorn] should be particularly effective in destroying the tradition of scientific folklore that depicts the artist as copying, more or less skillfully, the edible animals that he

> seriously meant to include in his list of kills. (André Leroi-Gourhan, *La grotte de Lascaux*, in J. Allain, *et al., Lascaux inconnu.*)

Lines crossing through the bodies of some of the animals are not images of the kill. The animals are represented in excellent health, quite plump even, and we can recognize females by the fact that they are gravid—just as the known figures of women are, with few exceptions, "big." This is hardly surprising in a society of hunters and gatherers: one cannot live on skinny animals, and that highly positive image is constant in rock art. It is equally clear in Paleolithic sculpture, whether we think of the Cap Blanc horses in Dordogne or the ones in the frieze of Roc-de-Sers in Charente. The reference to food is obviously paralleled by a symbolic construction.

The animal representations in Lascaux are not essentially different from those found in the whole group of caves on the French side of the Pyrenees. A strong tendency becomes apparent, clearly stated over the past century: the dominance of the animal theme in prehistoric art. When we make an inventory of the species represented and the situations in which the animals are placed, we realize that the iconographic resources make a finite whole. In the course of time, it is more or less the same animals that are represented and the same ones that are absent; for example, the carnivores present in Lascaux seemed rare for a long time, up to the discovery of the Chauvet Cave. Both in portable art (individual) and rock art (collective), all eras draw on a common source: their way of using themes and their diversity of associations enables us to sketch their evolution over the course of time.

The Unicorn has been described as a composite animal. But there are not always sharp borders between a composite creature, where one can clearly identify parts of several animals, and unidentified or apparently unknown animals. Similarly, when a bear is painted inside an aurochs, as in the Hall of Bulls in Lascaux, we can usually distinguish the two animals, whereas we would see a composite animal if the bear prolonged the aurochs. In representations where man and animal are associated, transitional forms are possible, and it is sometimes difficult to affirm that we are in the presence of an animal containing human elements or of a man with a sorcerer's mask. For example, as soon as an animal is represented standing up on two legs, it is called a sorcerer, but if it is standing on all four feet, with a slightly bizarre head, we don't see it as human. In fact, it seems that there is continuity in the transition from one animal species to another, or from animal to man, and this formal continuum, as well as the solutions adopted to represent the transition, constitute one of the characteristics of Paleolithic art. Thus men are associated with bison, or horned animals, in over 80% of cases; but seeing a sorcerer in the horned creature is a cultural projection that does not necessarily correspond to the practice of Paleolithic people. When one considers the decorated caves, the richness of the system resides in the communication between forms. Moreover, the distribution of these composite figures in space and time is clearly apparent: some caves have them, others don't.

Man as a whole, unconnected to animals, is absent from Lascaux. Did Paleolithic man represent himself by metaphor in the form of hybrid creatures, or was he forbidden to represent himself? The technical mastery attained in the animal figures could have worked equally well to depict a true human face or body. The reason he didn't do it, then, is because he restrained himself from doing it. "Perhaps he was only interested in animals, because unlike men, animals were out of his reach." (Georges

Bataille, *Oeuvres complètes*, IX.) In this still hostile world, where man has distanced himself from the animal condition, his symbolic and spiritual universe is entirely projected into the sublimated figure of the animal. Taking an "ecological" perspective, we may also think of the close proximity between human and animal societies, which were truly complementary, one nourishing and inspiring the other—the Animal still nourishing Man, literally and figuratively.

> The artists of the underground sanctuaries seem to have emphasized the complex relationships that unite animals to each other and the pitiful situation of man in the world. (…) Man, miserable and miniscule in the midst of swarming animals (…), is small, thrown over, pierced with arrows, or caricaturized; he is rarely completely human, but when he takes on more importance, he has become a bison-man, a deer-man, he has become a part of this animal world that lies at the center of his preoccupations. (Annette Laming-Emperaire, *La Signification de l'art rupestre paléolithique.*)

In composite animals and in the mixing of animal and human, we can see associations between species of living beings that eventually form a kind of pantheon. Certainly the bird-headed man of Lascaux, like the Unicorn, point us toward the oldest mythological structures, especially when the animals in these wall paintings can be found in the earliest forms of religion. It is not a question of seeing connections, but of recognizing the permanence of a common stock, used and reused with different functions according to the time and place.

We may say that groups of animal images are elements of communication utilized by symbolic thought but reappropriated according to an ecological and cultural context, which explains the diversity of caves, depending on times and regions. The particular ways elements are connected follow more or less invariable rules: we see fish associated with reindeer, but never with mammoth. However, whatever the recorded constants may be, our reading of the figures can only be general, as Annette Laming-Emperaire said as early as 1962:

> [The themes] may be mythical, recalling, for example, the origin and history of a given human group in its relationship with animal species; they may concretize a very ancient metaphysics and express a system of the world in which each species, animal or human, has its role to play (...); the themes may be religious and include supernatural beings. They may be all that at the same time—mythical, metaphysical and religious—but the distinctions we introduce between these different modes of thought may have little significance at the dawn of human thought. (Laming-Emperaire, *op. cit.*)

The Shaft: The Hidden Images

> *...Whoever has gone down there once is marked forever by that cry of silence.* (Philippe Sollers, *Tremblement de Bataille.)*

Why should the Shaft have a special place? After all, the whole cave is a sanctuary and exists because of all the paintings and engravings; but the Shaft seems to be a space more sacred than the rest, housing the representation of a scene the community as a whole was forbidden to see. Moreover, this representation has fascinated prehistorians and laymen alike and given rise to many interpretations.

What is called "the Shaft Scene" was described for the first time by Abbé Breuil in October, 1940 in his report to the Académie des Sciences:

The bottom of the shaft houses a more exceptional group. To the left a rhinoceros is trotting away from the scene; in the center, in black lines, a crudely sketched man is lying next to a spear and a spear-thrower; to the right, a bison outlined in black is watching him and seems to be losing his entrails like a horse disemboweled in a bull-fight. It seems to be the representation of a prehistoric drama. Near the man, a bird is perched on a pole—probably a totemic symbol or a funerary pole. (Henri Breuil, *Rapport lu à l'Académie des Inscriptions et Belles Lettres le 11 octobre 1940*, in Laval Léon *et al.*)

This description associates the different protagonists and objects depicted and organizes them into a scene; but it neglects what even the image reveals—the extremely intense character of the scene. In his commentary, Abbé Breuil sees here the relation of a dramatic hunting scene: the bison killed the man before being disemboweled by the rhinoceros, which then trots away. The object with a hook at one end and a cross-piece at the other at the bison's feet could be a spear-thrower; as for the pole crowned by a bird, he relates it to the "funerary poles of the Alaska Eskimos and the Vancouver Indians." Louis-René Nougier, another prehistorian, also constructs a narrative related to hunting, but a quite different one. He does not see the man as lying down, but standing up: he killed the bison and the pole shows that the animal belongs to him. "The lucky hunter of Lascaux who has defeated the bison will save it for a time of famine under a cairn that he will be able to identify under the snow by setting up the mast bearing his image." (Nougier, *Les Grottes préhistoriques ornées.*)

So the scene is taken as totally figurative, an attempt to bring back a moment in the daily life of the group. In this framework, where the painting is supposed to reproduce reality, some have evoked the shamanistic rites of Siberian populations, seeing the prone man as a shaman in an ecstatic trance and the bird on the stick as the vehicle that gives him a means of going to the sky; the man himself has something of the bird in him, as his head shows. The bisoon is seen as a sacrificed animal and the rhinoceros is not involved in the scene.

In his *Lascaux ou la naissance de l'art* (*Lascaux or the Birth of Art*), Georges Bataille, art historian, philosopher and writer, retained the religious idea of the shaman, but rejected the idea of a purely figurative scene. For him, the man who killed the bison has to atone for what Prehistoric man must have seen as a crime, since the separation between animal and human was not totally established at the time. "The author had to reject what was weighing on him because he had killed his victim: because of this act, he himself had fallen under the power of death and at the very least had to purify himself from an obvious stain." (G. Bataille, *Oeuvres complètes*, IX.) At the same time, he thought the rhinoceros was present to relieve the man of the crime: the arrow could not kill the bison and the rhinoceros disemboweled it. But precise studies have shown that the elements of the scene are not all contemporaneous. Bataille had also established a connection to the notion of sin, since the scene shows a living creature being sent from life to death. He was close to shamanism, in which one does not have the right to take life without an act or gesture of expiation. This is found in all animist societies of hunters and breeders, in which a ritual of restitution takes place when an animal is slaughtered, and this ritual was still alive in ancient Greece and Rome.

Other complementary interpretations point toward symbolism; they see in the masked men—and thus in the bird-headed man in the Shaft—characters from some Paleolithic mythology. Denis Vialou develops this point of view, recalling that outside of Lascaux, prehistoric men never represented a scene from life. He reads "the Shaft Scene" as

> the formulation of a myth of the life and death of the hunter. The presence of barbed and dotted signs, as in other places in Lascaux Cave, the bird sculpted on the spear-thrower, the rhinoceros, seemingly uninvolved in the tragedy, all reinforce the latter hypothesis: the apparent connection between the bison and the man is the sign of commemorative verisimilitude used by the artist to construct or reflect a mythical narrative that introduces the imaginary into the images and between them in a symbolic, non-visual way. (Denis Vialou, *La Préhistoire*.)

Historians have related the Shaft Scene to similar scenes existing in Assyrian calendars, and a bird-headed (falcon) man was the way the god Horus was represented in ancient Egypt. With the bird-headed man, as with the bull, we seem to be in the presence of deep, elementary myths, with animal species always present. The interpretation that orients the Shaft Scene towards a mythical narrative is enriched by associating it to the two back-to-back bison at the end of the Nave. These representations were both executed on a similar support of gold-yellow calcite. In both cases, a relationship is constructed between creatures, and—a remarkable fact—these scenes are located at two places in the cave that mark the boundary of two visual groups: on the one hand, a world that can be controlled, where man has left many traces, and on the other, a world beyond, dangerous and impenetrable.

Finally, only in Lascaux, in the Gabillou Cave (Sourzac, in Dordogne) and in the Trois-Frères Cave (Ariège), does one find male human beings with erections and masked heads, placed in a particular spot—here in a rather inaccessible spot, there in a tangled mass of figures. The bird-headed man is also present at Pech-Merle, Cougnac and Altamira. But only in Lascaux are these themes (the man and the wounded animal) so special in relation to the rest of the cave's visual arrangement; only here has a painter dramatized the death of a fellow human being. The painter has created not life—which is one of the possible interpretations of the works in the cave—but death, in a hidden place. Stocking death into memory: this is what human knowledge was experimenting with; and one can thus read this "Shaft Scene" as the expression of an important step in human self-awareness.

The Shaft: The Myth of Life and Death

A few enchanted animals and three sorcerers make up the quasi-totality of the Paleolithic documents (every one of them Magdalenian) attesting, in all likelihood, to underground magical practices; this is obviously not enough to turn to propitiatory magical rites when interpreting Paleolithic figurative iconography. Was the Bird-man, knocked down by the bison he had just disemboweled with his long spear, the victim of a spell cast by the sorcerer-artist who drew them in the Lascaux Shaft, or are the protagonists in this pictorial narrative actors in a mythogram? We hesitate as to whether we should see it as the illustration of a real-life story, the exorcism or the casting of an evil spell, or the formulation of a myth of the life and death of the hunter. The presence of barbed and dotted signs, as in other places in the Lascaux Cave, the bird sculpted on the spear-thrower, the rhinoceros, seemingly uninvolved in the tragedy, all reinforce the latter hypothesis: the apparent connection between the bison and the man is the sign of commemorative verisimilitude used by the artist to construct or reflect a mythical narrative that introduces the imaginary into the images and between them in a symbolic, non-visual way. Elsewhere on cave walls or objects, Paleolithic artists never projected real or possible life—that is, the story of the hunted hunter—into the figurative imaginary (for example, the presence of the rhinoceros, unique to Lascaux) and into the purely imaginary (the signs). In this respect, the dynamics of the mythogram painted in an isolated corner of Lascaux precedes the myths of Antiquity by many thousands of years, like a flash of genius projecting the shadows of living creatures, life and death and the original contradictions of beliefs onto the walls of the cavern. (Denis Vialou, *La Préhistoire.*)

The Quest for Signs

> *These graffiti "of obscure meaning" were interpreted as weapons, traps or huts, based on doubtful ethnographic comparisons; they were thought to be the expression of magical, votive or commemorative practices. Recognizing their place in an elaborate symbolic system of thought was totally out of the question. (*G. and S. Sauvet, A. Wlodarczyk, *Pour une sémiologie préhistorique.)*

From the very beginning of the twentieth century, without any discussion, French prehistorians considered the elements painted or engraved on the walls in various forms and equally present in portable art as "signs." They distinguished between animal figures, human figures, and "signs." They divided the representations: figurative ones were classified as art, the other, more or less abstract ones as signs with a meaning different from the rest of the pictorial representations. Today everyone agrees that topography, technique, form, and the study of the relationships among figures are useful tools for analysis; but from the moment the entity called "sign" is maintained as a pre-established category, a distinction is taken for granted that creates more problems than it solves. Some prehistorians say that an isolated hand is not a sign, but rather a segment of a human representation; they only confer the status of sign to something geometric, abstract, unidentified or unfinished, an outline, for example—in short, everything that would not allow us to slap a signification on an undefined form. But they refuse to put the representation of a headless animal in this category. Where, then, is the cut-off point? The quest for an order based on purely formal criteria would seem to lead to incoherence.

Similarly, the borderline between different categories of graphic elements turns out to be arbitrary: for some, a triangle pointing down is classified as "vulva" or "pubic triangle," whereas the same triangle pointing up is simply called "triangle." A barbed sign is never interpreted as a harpoon with a double row of barbs, although that is what it looks like, but as a male sexual sign. Besides, why shouldn't an isolated animal be a sign just as an abstract geometric representation is? Non-western prehistorians never interpret triangles as vulvas, for example, and in the category of icons, an Anglo-Saxon working in Australia will put a circle, a foot, a hand, a square, etc. in the same category.

Defined as they are by elimination, the signs have been studied in relation to other figured elements. In 1954, the prehistorian Annette Laming-Emperaire emphasized the association of certain signs with representations of animals of a clearly determined sex. She saw in them proof of the sexual meaning of the signs, and she classified them: for her, the circle and the oval, like the horse, correspond to the feminine; thin signs, and the bison, to the masculine order. But in the same time-period, using similar observations of signs and animals, André Leroi-Gourhan associated them in a totally opposite way. Both of them, however, agreed about the fact that "undeniably, the central theme of Paleolithic art is (…) a binary theme associating the horse with the bison or the wild ox, and this animal theme is reinforced by the signs, which occupy the same or a similar position." (André Leroi-Gourhan, *Les Religions de la préhistoire*.) We may also mention that a few years earlier, André Leroi-Gourhan (like Abbé Breuil) saw in the Lascaux Cave a sanctuary closely linked to hunting, which provided a clue for classifying everything:

> In the light of this hypothesis, everything can be explained and organized: the choice of difficult, far-off sites (thus favorable to religious mysteries); the topic of the representations, which is always game—game to be killed in order to feed or defend the tribe. Those strange-looking signs are arrows, spear-throwers, spears, various kinds of branches; those complicated triangles, those checkerboard figures often painted on the very flanks of the animals, or in front of them, sometimes at their feet, could easily be snares or traps. The dots may have the same meaning. (Laming-Emperaire and Roussel, *La Grotte de Lascaux*.)

If certain signs are singled out and interpreted as sexual symbols while others are perceived as being more or less figurative, this would mean that at the time of Lascaux anyone could read anything at all in a figure. It would then be nearly impossible to recognize a system that allowed the communication of symbols among individuals at any given time.

By considering everything that was not figurative, other prehistorians saw in the abstract symbols a coherent system, forming a kind of writing. It is highly probable that the signs were placed on the walls of the caves or on objects to transmit something to the people who looked at them. Yet they do not fulfill the criteria for the existence of writing: they do not appear in a linear chain, whether horizontal or vertical, in Lascaux or elsewhere.

If, in Lascaux or any decorated cave, we agree to see a symbolic system in which everything represented has the value of a sign, we can study the alternance between the figurative and the non-figurative, taking as analytical factors shape, color, technique, and the whole topographical arrangement. This classification assumes that instead of studying combinations between animals and signs, we consider, in Lascaux and elsewhere, that everything painted and engraved created a system; then we could try to see how all the elements in the cave were associated to create a meaning.

We must also keep in mind that the paintings and engravings of Lascaux Cave were elaborated at different periods, and that 5,000 years may have passed between the first and the last. The study of the superimposition and erasing of figures might enable us to understand how their combinations were made and modified, how the signs changed over the course of time, how the symbols were manipulated, etc.

Also, when we take their geographic distribution into account, the signs show some regionalization. We can identify the limits of a territory and at the same time assume that groups could communicate with common elements. For example, the roof-shaped signs (hence the term "tectiform") are strictly localized: the typical shapes are found in four caves in Perigord, in four others in the Cantabrian mountain area of Spain, and then in the Lot region and the Pyrenees. The signs called "hut-like", the one in Lascaux long called "the great sorcerer," for example, are also extremely localized. Transmitting these elements to others must have been indispensable for the groups' stability and survival.

This point of view would take better account of the complexity of meanings of prehistoric art. This art, which preceded structured languages and forms of writing, was based on a complex association of perceived objects and emotions rather than on elements of narrative structure. This is exactly why rock art represents a memory; we are dealing here with oral transmission, more with myth than language. We can speak of a memory whose primary function is to determine the groups individuals belong to, the territories they occupy, the rules of kinship that determine inter-personal relationships; and this type of memory only appears at the beginning of the Upper Paleolithic, with modern man. The idea of mythological structure implies that to read these figures, an actor or witness is indispensable; this takes us out of the realm of writing.

The Cave, a Symbolic Place

> *The cave appears to be (…) a truly organized world. We cannot see the details of the symbolic system, but we feel that it is based on representations whose organization presupposes a way of thinking that goes well beyond the preconceived ideas we have of it. (*André Leroi-Gourhan, *Les Religions de la préhistoire.)*

Even before looking at the paintings and engravings of Lascaux, we may wonder about the attraction the cave held for men of the Paleolithic. Why should they go there to do something they could have done—and in fact did—just as well in the open, on rocky walls and on objects of everyday life (weapons, tools, adornments)? What is special about the cavern that no other space can have, and is it only a question of space?

Since the beginning of the historic period in both western and eastern societies, founding narratives and myths show that the cave constantly played a symbolic role, whether associated with mystery (of magic or the sacred), or taken to be a religious or initiatory space—that is, a space of knowledge. It was often perceived as the womb of the world and the cosmos in miniature, a dark universe lit by inner light. It has been considered as the birthplace of gods and heroes: Agni in the *Rig-Veda* of India, Abraham in Arab legends, and Jesus are said to have been born in a cave; it is also the abode of nymphs and monsters, as in Homer's *Odyssey*: the seductive Calypso and Polyphemus the Cyclops killed by Odysseus.

The cavern is the threshold between the visible and the invisible, the living and divinities, the real and the imaginary. It is symbolically a *passage*. Originally, the words for it indicated its characteristics: the French *antre* (Greek *antron*) suggested the disquieting underground lair of beasts, like *cavern* (Latin *caverna*, derived from *cavus*, "hollow"), whereas *grotto* (Greek *kruptê*) applied only to an underground passage. It is a cellar, the French cave (*cavus*) and also a crypt (*kruptê*), a place for storage and meditation rather than shelter, a sacred hollow devoted both to collective gatherings and the activity of the artist. It may indeed have served as a spartan refuge (a cell) for the monks and hermits of Christendom, but it was also a space decorated with infernal and astronomical images, designed to impress the minds of the adepts of ancient mystery religions.

The poets and philosophers of ancient Greece had different readings of the cave. For Plato, it was an allegorical space

(*Republic, VII*), the pretext for a reflection on the visible and the virtual, the light of knowledge and the darkness of ignorance. In the work of Homer, it had symbolic value: his description of the Cave of the Nymphs on the island of Ithaca gives us the vision of a primal place of abundance where life is woven and mortals and immortals meet:

> Phorkys, the old sea baron, has a cove
> here in the realm of Ithaka; two points
> of high rock, breaking sharply, hunch around it,
> making a haven from the plunging surf
> that gales at sea roll inward. Deep inside,
> at mooring range, good ships can ride unmoored.
> There, on the inmost shore, an olive tree
> throws wide its boughs over the bay; nearby
> a cave of dusky light is hidden
> for those immortal girls, the Naiades.
> (*Odyssey* XIII, Fitzgerald translation.)

The space of the cave probably never belonged to the same category as the domestic spaces where everyone has his or her assigned place. It is set inside nature, with the attributes specific to nature, in such a way that men simply could not ritualize it with the same rigor as the sacred spaces of hearth and home. There is good reason to think that the cave is something other than the representation of the world constituted by the home.

Indeed, the cave is a world that psychoanalysts have identified as a privileged place for individual expressions around the myth indispensable for every social group—a founding myth, perhaps. We can assume that the men of the Paleolithic were extremely sensitive to the opposition of night/day, light/darkness, and that duality may have found its expression in creative underground activity. One prehistorian, Michel Lorblanchet, has attempted to identify the totality of human interventions in this space, which itself is loaded with meanings.

> The representations are never outside of the rock—which makes the term "support" particularly inadequate. The cave is truly a participant: it takes on life under the thrust of its inner relief. Art animates the cavern; we have to wonder if the harmony between cave and creator comes only from formal interplay or if it does not primarily have a symbolic function. The priest-artist of the Ice Ages awakes latent images, creatures asleep in the rock, with a life-giving gesture. In the cave, womb of the earth, he was, no doubt, presiding over the birth of the world and communicating with the world of spirits. (Michel Lorblanchet, *Les Grottes ornées de la préhistoire*.)

As an intermediary between the world of the living and the world of the dead, between the real and the imaginary, the cave was itself in a kind of time that has no chronology. Taking the darkness of the cave as a place for expression meant shutting out the daylight world for a while—the world where time is perceptible through the movement of the sun, the seasons, etc. It meant going into the only neutralized, accessible space to express one's emotions and thus abolish the passage of time; but by doing so, this place in which one could get out of measurable time also became the place where elements of memory could be inscribed, and seen: mythological themes and techniques transmitted by one's ancestors.

Lascaux and the Origin of Art

Some prehistorians have always refused to talk about prehistoric "art": for them, paintings and engravings were exclusively tied to religion, whereas art could only exist independently from that relationship, defined only by esthetic pleasure. If we reject the word *art* when the production of a work depends on the supernatural, we exclude a large quantity of works, but even without arguing over the content of such a division, it is hard to see why the people of Lascaux should not have been sensitive to beauty.

A part of Paleolithic painting has always been seen as the result of visions from a shamanistic trance (see Clottes and Lewis-William, *Les Chamanes de la préhistoire, Transe et magie dans les grottes ornées,* La Maison des Roches, 2001.) But visions are an ephemeral phenomenon, whereas the painted and engraved works of art—which cannot be dissociated—form, as they do in Lascaux, extremely complex wholes, linked to various aspects of life, both social and individual. Rock art has also been interpreted as the highest expression of man's struggle against a hostile environment, its appearance marking a change in his relationship to nature. This was the art historian Max Raphael's theory, which was taken up later, with variants:

> After all, if wall paintings strike us by their modernity, so much so that they seem familiar, it is because they are the product of very specific historical conditions, and have, for this reason, a strong symbolic significance in relation to all spiritual and moral creation: they appeared at the precise moment when humanity began to dominate animals instead of being dominated by them. This liberation found its artistic expression, as strong and universal as Greek art

> when Greece freed itself from agriculture to turn to naval commerce, and abandoned an existence exclusively bound to the earth, to enter into the social and political life of the city. (Max Raphaël, *Trois essais sur la signification de l'art pariétal.*)

Human beings' distancing themselves from animals would thus be one aspect of the "Paleolithic revolution" and even more so, of the upheavals in the Upper Paleolithic. Among other data, we should state that men developed blade production, which, after hand-axes and flint-knapping, favors the diversification and specialization of implements; at the same time, they were beginning to use bones to make tools. These social changes are accompanied by diverse symbolic manifestations: ornaments, jewelry, paintings and engravings on different supports.

This point of view leads us to a different perception of the question of the origins of prehistoric art, and thus of the place of Lascaux. The origin of man certainly takes place in a biological framework, but the appearance of technology—work—about four million years ago enables us to insert the origin of art into the history of human thought, with stages in the formalization of memory. Tools were at first instruments for acting on nature, but with something more than mere material results. From the moment human beings struck two flints together to obtain more or less specialized tools, they were constructing something symbolic: they were trying to reproduce an object, to make tools that all had roughly the same shape. Technology immediately transmitted the memory of gestures, tools, shapes, and rules among individuals, groups and generations. We have here a cumulative memory of the material realm that modified the evolution of human lineage, transforming its capacities to learn and act. These technological objects generated social relationships—men became specialized, exchanged, etc.—and at the same time went beyond utilitarian purposes: tools were manufactured from various materials, sometimes collected far from their habitat not because the material was more efficient but to change the color or aspect of the tool.

This kind of production was intended for action, but had symbolic value. When it spread, we may suppose that products for display began to appear: ornaments for the body and hair, body painting, which—along with dance and music—are linked both to the body and to social mobility. These elements, like the decoration of weapons and tools, give genuine information, a kind of traveling information, alongside of rock art, which is a stationary kind of information. Very early in human history, cultural systems existed with their social meaning; the next steps—the formalization of languages and writing—are not far off. From the first steps on, everything was there: sacred spaces and objects, the appropriation of nature, of what people wear and acquire, the inscription in a territory. We may ask ourselves if the need and demand for art, which appeared before they were conceptualized, are not constituent elements of the human species.

The Emergence of Art

The emergence of figurative art in the strict sense of the term about 35 or 40,000 years ago, on both rock walls and objects, where figuration and abstraction coexist from the very start, cannot appear as a complete "revolution," still less as an "explosion." In art, as well as in tools and ways of life, the Upper Paleolithic's break with what preceded it is far from complete. Rather it seems to be a progressive change, since, as far as we can see today, there is no "cradle of art": the emergence of art is a scattered phenomenon, disseminated all over the planet through tens of thousands of years. For some parts of the world, we can even envision appearances, disappearances and reappearances of the artistic phenomenon, successively taking on different forms and styles without the slightest connection between them. The beginning of the Upper Paleolithic essentially brought in a quantitative change, marked by an increase in the number of signs of symbolic behavior, such as the proliferation of geometric markings and lines on bone and stone, the multiplication of ornaments and tombs that express a general increase of ritual activity and beliefs relative to human destiny.

On the other hand, an unquestionably qualitative change takes place with the appearance of figurative rock art: that is, with the development on rocky walls, outside or in cavities, of identifiable images referring to the surrounding physical world, often accompanied by geometric motifs. The material support changes and the themes become considerably more diversified. The existence of rock art has not been proven in any region of the world before 40,000 BP. This change may appear spectacular: above all, it essentially seems to reflect a modification of mental structures, a change in belief systems. (Lorblanchet, *La naissance de l'art, 1999.*)

Lascaux, Time and Memory

When we try to interpret the artworks of Lascaux, what is accessible to us? Perhaps we should primarily base our interpretations on lived experience and the memory of lived experience. We do not mean codified memory—recorded, as we know it—but something that has to do with experience to be transmitted by the senses. That is probably why this sense of the past is still available to us, composed of emotional elements before being anything else, elements inseparable from the cultural life of Paleolithic society. We may say that this is where the essential aspects of the hunter-gatherers' preoccupations lay: at the very early stages of culture, they turned to painting and engraving to record and transmit manifestations of an esthetic nature—visual, auditory, etc.—as well as manifestations of a reproductive nature (sexuality is present.) Thus the fundamental elements of what it means to be human are present in Paleolithic culture, just as they are in the structuring of the individual.

We must not forget how we distort time when we look into the past, in the same way that psychoanalysis can put together the events in an individual's history at a given moment in his or her life by suppressing the linearity of time. It is a difficult problem in archeology: events contemporary to each other are never studied separately, and even cultural diversity is erased. In the traces men have left, however important they may be (as in Lascaux), we see only what has evolved—relative positions in time. In other words, our reconstruction leads us in the end to reconstitute an evolution, and anything tangled, any non-linear structure, is flattened out in this scale of long duration. Whereas it would be important to know what the perception of time and cycles of time was for the people of Lascaux and Paleolithic societies in general. Did it stretch beyond the life of a generation, of an individual? How did they perceive ancestors and filiation? If we only took as models the hunter-gatherer societies described by contemporary ethnologists, we would answer that time for Prehistoric people was the time of subsistence, thus of seasons, and this cyclical time is always preeminent compared to duration.

However, the discovery of the Cussac Cave (Dordogne) in 2000 enables us to rethink the question of time. There, the works of art form a homogeneous whole: the figures were traced rapidly, perhaps in a few hours, by a few people. Then the cave was closed and neither animals nor men returned. As for its contents, Cussac is unique to this day. The men there represented many animals and buried about ten individuals. In the open caves, there are no sepultures to be found—the bodies were simply laid on the ground and became the prey of carnivores in a few hours. If there was a decision to make the sepultures inviolable and preserve the integrity of the relationship between the figures on the walls and the phenomenon of sepultures, that would imply another dimension of the work of memory. The question of time would come up here not in terms of the individual, but of the group, because there was collective action. We may imagine that systems of noting time—or more precisely, as Francesco Errico says, "artificial memory systems"—existed for the people of Lascaux and their contemporaries.

"Artificial Memory Systems"

Like the other decorated Paleolithic caves, Lascaux enables us to perceive an organized world, a collective imaginary based on structured, symbolic connections and cross-references. So rich a mental organization implies the existence of a space and time experienced both individually and socially. These men already had interiorized "calendars or systems of notation," reflections of individual participation in collective life and memory. (…)

Man is the only being able to create artificial memory systems, that is, means of recording, transmitting and processing information outside of his own body. Among these systems, writing is probably the one that has most conditioned the development of the majority of human societies, at least

since the adoption of printing. Yet many other artificial memory systems were used before writing. Their nature and the implications of their use on the biological and cultural evolution of human populations have not yet been explored with the attention they deserve.
Francesco d'Errico, *L'Art gravé azilien*, 1994.

The phenomenon of superimposition on cave walls, perfectly visible in Lascaux, cannot be interpreted outside of the problem of time, since superimpositions hardly exist in portable art, although a few thin engraved slabs in La Marche and Limeuil are sometimes held to be exceptions. The distinction between portable art, tied to one person, and rock art, supposedly collective, leads to many questions. Does the collective character come from the fact that it exists in the neutralized space of the cave, as opposed to domestic space? Or because we find superimpositions in it, because it is always in a state of transformation, because it is restructured as additions are made? Wall scraping, graffiti, would then be included in rock art.

We can easily see many stages of execution in the cave, but cannot feel the thickness of time; we don't know if the accumulation of gestures came from the same people, from different people or from whole groups. All that remains today is the result of that work of memory, or of that expression of a memory: was it born from an intention, or is it the chance production of the superimposition of artworks? For the people of Lascaux, memory might have been felt as a kind of whole. At any rate, memory was experienced underground, the only place where one could escape from time.

27

THE AXIAL PASSAGE, THE APSE

29

30

31

32

THE NAVE

37

39

The Lateral Passage, The Apse

Small horse, engraved and painted in black, preserved in a hollow protected from erosion on the right wall of the Lateral Passage (27.) Left wall of the Lateral Passage: detail of the body of a small engraved horse whose paint has disappeared. This animal is represented on both sides of a rocky outjutting that prevents viewing the whole animal all at once (28.)

Detail of a red deer's head engraved on the blackened wall of the Apse amid a tangle of engraved lines (29.)

On the panel of the Footprint, the central horse (the stallion) shows a hide striped with engraved arrows (30.) The bison at the right end is superimposed on a horse. Both are striped with lines (31.)

The Nave

The Black Cow is superimposed on a frieze of horses. This panel is reminiscent of the Axial Passage by its composition and the style of the animals (32.)

The "coats of arms" are brightly colored checkerboard signs at the level of the Black Cow's hooves (33.)

Detail of the little horses' heads emerging from behind the Black Cow (34.)

Right wall of the Nave: the first three red deer, traced with manganese, in the frieze of the "swimming red deer" (35.)

The back-to-back bison occupy a little calcite-covered alcove at the bottom of the Nave, by the entrance to the narrow hallway leading to the Chamber of Felines (36.)

The Chamber of Felines and the Shaft

Engravings at the entrance to the Chamber of Felines where one can discern, among other tracings, a horse seen front view and a feline profile (37.)

Detail of the Shaft scene, located to the right of the rhinoceros not included in the photograph (38.)

Forequarters of a horse represented in the Shaft on the wall facing the preceding scene (39.)

LASCAUX TODAY

In places where harmonies rang out and vanished long ago, countless cracks, the sole survivors of the destruction of time, will never give us the illusion of the original sound.
*(*Claude Lévi-Strauss, *Anthropologie Structurale,* Plon, 1958.*)*

The decorated prehistoric caves and shelters are a very fragile heritage; only part of it has survived into the present time. Rock art, a common phenomenon in many societies for tens of thousands of years, is abundantly represented in the world, as the number of sites preserved on all continents is estimated at 400,000 (see Jean Clottes, *Le Musée des roches.*) Several large concentrations of rock art sites are on UNESCO's list of "the heritage of humanity"—including the Paleolithic caves of the Vézère Valley in France, Lascaux among them.

The sites that have been preserved had to resist the repeated assaults of weather and people alike; countless sites were wrecked, their treasures lost forever. Lascaux, Chauvet, Cosquer, Cussac and many others remained inaccessible for thousands of years in stable environments, which evolved very slowly and consequently did not lead to the degradation of the works of art.

From the start of the twentieth century, tourists were immediately interested by the first discoveries of the decorated

Paleolithic caves, and this interest has never waned. Except for a few rare examples of judicious resistance and refusal of economic exploitation in order to leave the sites as they were found, most caves were made accessible to visitors and more or less fitted up to meet their needs. But contradictory interests appeared very early: scientific knowledge of rock art conflicted with the transformation of the caves for tourists.

After its discovery in 1940, the Lascaux Cave was unrestrainedly accommodated for tourists before any scientific study could be made, despite warnings from specialists. A steady flow of tourists visited it from July 1948 on; the successive modifications of its floor and entrance had the sole objective of making it easier for the increasing number of visitors to walk around. Lascaux had more than 1,000 visitors a day at the beginning of the sixties! The cave was definitively closed to the public in 1963 after biological and climatic imbalance began to alter the painted walls. Only then—at last!—were scientists able to intervene in Lascaux. In the first period, the specialists in the committee immediately created by André Malraux, then Minister of Culture, had to respond to emergencies as diverse as the study of its geology, hydrology, and underground climate. And microorganisms had begun to proliferate dangerously, due to the excessive number of visitors that had drastically transformed the cave's atmosphere.

Only the return to a stable situation, at the beginning of the eighties, allowed teams of archeologists to begin their work. Ever since Lascaux was closed, they had been obliged to make do with data accumulated before them, often under bad conditions, like the readings Abbé Glory was able to take when the cave was being fitted up in 1957-58. Despite these constraints, a huge synthetic, multidisciplinary work was published in 1979: *Lascaux inconnu (The Unknown Lascaux)*; today it is still the only available reference work that brings together the knowledge of dozens of specialists. It condemns the dramatic loss of information about the archeological context that occurred after the floors and deposits were destroyed throughout the cave when air-conditioning equipment was installed.

Lascaux has gone through a period of imbalance in its underground environment since 2001, a continuation of the disturbances observed in 1962-63, which for a while were thought to be under control. After decades of apparent stability, microorganisms (a fungus and a bacterium) developed again on the floors and clayey outcroppings at the foot of the decorated walls. What caused this imbalance? Probably a steady accumulation of many causes until an aggravating factor triggered the process of deterioration; but we have every right to think that Lascaux is still energetically resisting after half a century of attacks.

The present scientific committee, appointed by the Minister of Culture in July 2002, has the task of finding appropriate treatments to destroy the microorganisms, and also to find a way of restoring the natural equilibrium of the cave inside its environment. Indeed, Lascaux should not remain dependent on artificial conditions indefinitely; it is preferable to approximate the climatic and biological conditions that characterize the underground environments natural to decorated caves—all the more so when they are modest in size, like Lascaux, Font-de-Gaume or Altamira.

The decorated caves are closed to the public, but now facsimiles are being made to compensate for their closure. The first was Lascaux II, built in 1983 near the original cave, followed by the recreation of the paintings of the Niaux Cave, in the Pyrenean Park of Prehistory in Tarascon-sur-Ariège and by the copy of Altamira in Spain. The creation of replicas continues to improve; it is a perfect response to the demands of a growing public. Today Lascaux has close to 400,000 visitors a year, and the replica of Altamira has even more. The progress in the techniques of communication used in these educational replicas enables visitors to capture something of the practice and intentions of prehistoric artists, all the more so as the facsimile faithfully restores part of the paintings next to the original site in tones somewhat faded by time. In this way, the replica not only answers the need for knowledge of an eager public, but seems to be the basis for any realistic policy of protection of the caves for future generations.

BIBLIOGRAPHY

To learn more about Lascaux

In English:

WINDELS Fernand, *The Lascaux Cave Paintings,* Faber and Faber, London.

In French:

ALLAIN Jacques et LEROI-GOURHAN Arlette (sous la direction de), *Lascaux inconnu,* éd. du CNRS, 1979, en particulier : Allain Jacques, *L'industrie lithique et osseuse de Lascaux,* Delluc Brigitte et Gilles, *L'éclairage,* Couraud Claude et Laming-Emperaire Annette, *Les colorants,* Leroi-Gourhan André, *La Nef et le Diverticule des félins* et *Les animaux et les signes,* Vialou Denis, *Le Passage et l'Abside.*

ALLEMAND Luc, *Qui sauvera Lascaux ?* in *La Recherche,* n°363, avril 2003.

AUJOULAT Norbert, *Lascaux. Le rôle du déterminisme culturel : des modalités d'élection du site aux protocoles de construction des édifices graphiques pariétaux,* Thèse, Bordeaux I, 2002.

AUJOULAT Norbert, GENESTE Jean-Michel, RIGAUD Jean-Philippe, ROUSSOT Alain, *La Vézère des origines,* Imprimerie nationale, 1991, en particulier N. Aujoulat, *La Grotte de Lascaux.*

BREUIL Henri, *400 siècles d'art pariétal, Les cavernes ornées de l'âge du renne,* Centre d'études et de documentation préhistoriques, Montignac, 1952.

CLOTTES Jean, *Retour à Lascaux,* in *Préhistoire passion,* La Maison des roches, 2003.

Collectif. *L'art des cavernes : atlas des grottes ornées paléolithiques françaises.* Avant-propos d'André Leroi-Gourhan, Imprimerie nationale, 1984, en particulier André Leroi-Gourhan, *Grotte de Lascaux.*

DEMOULE Jean-Paul, *Lascaux,* in *Les France, 2. Traditions,* Gallimard, collection Quarto, 1997 (1992).

LAMING-EMPERAIRE Annette et ROUSSEL Monique, *La Grotte de Lascaux,* Caisse Nationale des Monuments Historiques, Paris, 1950.

LAMING-EMPERAIRE Annette, *Lascaux, peintures et gravures,* éditions Voici, Science-information, 1964 (1959 en anglais).

LORBLANCHET Michel, *La Naissance de l'art, Genèse de l'art préhistorique dans le monde,* éditions errance, 1999.

VIALOU Denis, *La Préhistoire,* Gallimard, l'Univers des formes, 1991.

To learn more about prehistoric times

In English:

KNECHT H., PIKE-TAY, A. and WHITE, R. (eds.), *Before Lascaux: a Complex Record of the Early Upper Paleolithic*, CRC Press, 1993.

WHITE Randall, *Prehistoric Art: the Symbolic Journey of Humankind*, H.N. Abrams, New York, 2003.

In French:

AUJOULAT N., GENESTE J.-M., ARCHAMBEAU C., DELLUC M., DUDAY H., HENRY-GAMBIER D., *La Grotte ornée de Cussac, Le Buisson-de-Cadouin (Dordogne) : premières observations,* B.S.P.F., tome 99, n°1, p.129-153, 2002.

BOUCHER DE PERTHES Jacques, *Antiquités celtiques et antédiluviennes, Mémoire sur l'industrie primitive et les arts à leur origine,* Treuttel et Würtz, 3 vol. (1847, 1857, 1864).

CARTAILHAC Émile, *L'Âge de la pierre dans les souvenirs et superstitions populaires,* C. Reinwald & Cie, 1877.

CARTAILHAC Émile, *La France préhistorique, d'après les sépultures et les monuments,* Félix Alcan, 1889.

CARTAILHAC Émile, «*Les cavernes ornées de dessins. La grotte d'Altamira, Espagne. Mea culpa d'un sceptique*», in *L'Anthropologie*, 1902, t. 13 ; repris in Richard Nathalie, *L'invention de la préhistoire (Anthologie),* Presses Pocket, 1992.

CHALMIN Émilie, *Caractérisation des oxydes de manganèse et usage des pigments noirs au Paléolithique supérieur,* (Thèse de Doctorat, 2004).

CLOTTES Jean, *Le Musée des roches. L'art rupestre dans le monde*, Le Seuil, 2000.

CLOTTES Jean (sous la direction de), *La Grotte Chauvet, l'art des origines,* Le Seuil, 2001.

CUVIER Georges, *Recherches sur les ossements fossiles où l'on rétablit les caractères de plusieurs espèces d'animaux que les révolutions du globe paraissent avoir détruits. Discours préliminaires (1812),* éditions GF-Flammarion, Présentation, notes et chronologie par Pierre Pellegrin.

DELPORTE Henri, *L'Image des animaux dans l'art préhistorique,* Picard, 1990.

D'ERRICO Francesco, *L'art gravé azilien. De la technique à la signification,* XXXIe supplément à *Gallia Préhistoire,* CNRS éditions, 1994.

DUCROS Albert, DUCROS Jacqueline et JULIAN Frédéric (sous la direction de), *La culture est-elle naturelle ? Histoire, épistémologie et applications récentes du concept de culture,* éditions errance, 1999.

GROENEN Marc, *Pour une histoire de la préhistoire. Le Paléolithique.* Jérôme Millon, Grenoble, 1994.

JÈGUES WOLKIEWIEZ Chantal, *Une appréhension de l'art préhistorique grâce à l'ethno-astronomie,* in Mallory J., *Séminaires 2000-2001,* éditions Polaires, 2002.

JOUANNET François, *« Antiquités gauloises »,* in *Calendrier des corps administratifs, judiciaires et militaires de la Dordogne,* Périgueux, 1818.

LAMING-EMPERAIRE Annette, *La Signification de l'art rupestre paléolithique,* Picard, 1962.

LAMING-EMPERAIRE Annette, *Origines de l'archéologie préhistorique en France, Des superstitions médiévales à la découverte de l'homme fossile*, Picard, 1964.

LEROI-GOURHAN André, *Préhistoire de l'art occidental,* Genève, Mazenod, 1965.

LEROI-GOURHAN André, *Les religions de la préhistoire*, P.U.F., 1971 (1955).

LEROI-GOURHAN André, *Le Fil du temps. Ethnologie et préhistoire, 1935-1970*, Fayard, 1983.

LORBLANCHET Michel, *Les grottes ornées de la préhistoire : nouveaux regards,* éditions errance, 1995.

MORTILLET Gabriel et Adrien, *La Préhistoire, origine et antiquité de l'homme,* Bibliothèque des sciences contemporaines, Schleicher frère, sans date [1910, préface], édition augmentée de Mortillet Gabriel, *Le Préhistorique, Antiquité de l'homme,* C. Reinwald, 1883.

NOUGIER Louis-René, *Les grottes préhistoriques ornées, de France, d'Espagne et d'Italie,* Balland, 1990.

RAPHAËL Max, *Trois essais sur la signification de l'art pariétal paléolithique* (trad. sous la direction de Patrick Brault), éditions Le couteau sous la plaie/Kronos, Limoges, 1986.

ROUSSOT Alain, *L'art préhistorique,* Sud-Ouest université, Bordeaux, 1997.

SAUVET Georges et Suzanne, WLODARCZYK André, *Essai de sémiologie préhistorique (Pour une théorie des premiers signes graphiques de l'homme)*, in *Bulletin de la Société préhistorique française,* tome 74, 1977.

STIEGLER Bernard, *La Technique et le temps, 1. La faute d'Épiméthée,* Galilée, 1994.

PHOTOGRAPHIC CREDITS:

For all photographs: Jean-Michel Geneste, Service Régional de l'Archéologie d'Aquitaine, Ministère de la Culture. All rights reserved.

CREDITS FOR THE ILLUSTRATIONS:

14, 15, 16: Jean-Paul Lhomme, Service Régional de l'Archéologie (SRA), DRAC d'Aquitaine. 66: Jean-Paul Lhomme (SRA), after B. and G. Delluc, "L'éclairage," in Allain J. and Leroi-Gourhan A., *Lascaux inconnu.* 70: Jean-Paul Lhomme (SRA), after C. Couraud and A. Laming-Emperaire, "Les colorants" in *op. cit.* 62, 63, 64, 65: Jean-Paul Lhomme (SRA), after J. Allain, "L'industrie lithique et osseuse de Lascaux," in *op.cit.* 72, 73: Jean-Michel Geneste.

Printed on the first day
of summer 2004
on Contraste 150 g and Alpaca 250 g
from Papeteries de Condat
on the presses of France quercy
in cahors
for éditions fanlac
near la Tour Vésone
in Périgueux
www.fanlac.com